HEA NCES

The Author

Now in his early sixties Howard Booth has been involved in pastoral work in busy urban areas for almost forty years. He is now based in a rural part of Dorset where he combines oversight of a small group of churches with a wider responsibility for promoting health and healing ministries throughout the Methodist Church.

Previous publications include *Prayer Tools for Health and Healing* (The Grail) and *Stepping Stones to Christian Maturity* (BRF). Recently he edited a Workbook entitled *In Search of Health and Wholeness* which had been prepared by a Working Party set up by the Methodist Division of Social Responsibility, from whose London office it can be obtained (1 Central Buildings, Westminster, SW1H 9NH).

He is associated with the Churches' Council for Health and Healing and general enquiries about such ministries can be addressed to the Council at St Marylebone Parish Church, Marylebone Road, London, NW1 5LT.

HOWARD BOOTH

HEALING EXPERIENCES

A devotional and study guide

the bible reading fellowship

The Bible Reading Fellowship
St Michael's House
2 Elizabeth Street
London SW1W 9RQ

First published 1985

British Library CIP data

Booth, Howard
    Healing experiences : a devotional and study guide.
    1. Devotional calendars
    I. Title   II. Bible Reading Fellowship
    242'.2   BV4810

    ISBN 0–900164–66–2

Cover photo: Nicholas Servian/Woodmansterne

Printed by Bocardo & Church Army Press Ltd, Cowley, Oxford, England

CONTENTS

ACKNOWLEDGEMENTS

My thanks to Canon Raymond Hammer, Director of the Bible Reading Fellowship, for inviting me to undertake this task. I would also like to thank the members of a Methodist Division of Social Responsibility Working Party with whom I have been reflecting on these issues. Our meetings have made me think much harder about many of the issues associated with health and healing than I would otherwise have done.

The people at Trinity Methodist Church, Workington, and other Workington Methodists have given me considerable encouragement and support. I write this as my ministry among them is drawing to a close and as I prepare to undertake a wider task in encouraging the study of health and healing ministries in the Methodist Church at large. I shall always be grateful for their friendship and help. It has been a privilege to spend this one period of my active ministry among them and so close to the mountains and fells of Cumbria.

H.B.

INTRODUCTION

We usually think that we have experienced healing when we recover from an illness or any injury. We cut a finger whilst carving a joint of meat and, providing we keep it clean and disinfected, it heals. We have an operation to remove a diseased appendix and, after a period of convalescence, the wounds, internal and external, begin to heal and we get back to how we were before we felt the pain. We have an infectious illness and, following upon a course of anti-biotics, we recover.

But healing is an experience with much wider implications. In his study of the modern hospital which arose out of his being invited to examine the role of the hospital chaplain, Dr Michael Wilson tells us that he came to the following conclusion about the primary task of the hospital: It is 'to enable patients, their families and staff to learn from the experience of illness and death how to build a healthy society'. He also came to believe that health is . . . 'being able to respond in a mature way to life as it is'. (See *The Hospital — A Place of Truth*, University of Birmingham.)

Michael Wilson (who is both priest and doctor) glimpsed a vision of a modern hospital as being more than a health factory repairing damaged bodies. He recognized the significance of the delicate mass of human relationships which constitute the modern health and healing scene and recognized their healing potential. He also saw how those relationships were seldom fully used and indeed were often abused. He came to believe that healing experiences and renewed health are not delivered by technological expertise alone but need the insights of the 'art of healing' in which both healers and those being healed discover a greater 'wholeness'.

Medical Developments

The massive improvements in general health in the developed world owe a great deal to the public health measures which, in the United Kingdom, began in the early years of this present century. Then came greatly improved services in ante-natal care and obstetrics which reduced deaths in child-birth to miniscule proportions. There followed the infection fighters which, beginning with the sulphonomides in the late twenties and continuing with the dramatic discovery of penicillin by Alexander Fleming in 1928, outlawed many of the most feared infectious diseases. Surgical and anaesthetic techniques also continued to develop and improve until we come to the present era of plastic surgery and organ transplants.

Psychological medicine also made considerable strides and there are now many therapeutic drugs which help to relieve the sufferings of the seriously mentally ill (the psychotics) and the ever-increasing numbers of people who suffer from what is popularly known as 'nerves' (the neurotics). Some illnesses once thought to have a physical cause are now seen to be psychosomatic in their origins and need to be treated by a combination of psychological and physical means. Indeed all illnesses are best treated by those with psychological insights so that the relationships involved can facilitate the healing process. This is much more than a good 'bedside manner'; it is concerned to develop a healthy kind of trust which encourages the acceptance of responsibility by the patient and facilitates growth even in crises.

The spiritual factor

Dr Kenneth Keek is a medical historian. In *Medicine, Morals and Man*, he refers to the dramatic progress that has been made and then goes on . . . 'So successful indeed, that we have run into the danger of treating the patient's physical and chemical state rather than the human being'. He reminds us that the psychologists and psychiatrists have helped to restore the balance but this leaves one neglected area, namely that of inspiration and motivation, which are the areas of life covered by religious faith. He even suggests somewhat audaciously: 'It could be the future task of medicine to restore the creative fields of religious emotions so sadly and unnecessarily depressed by the tree of knowledge'.

A healthy combination

This book is designed to help groups and individuals to think about the issues involved in discovering a more effective personal and corporate 'wholeness'. I have drawn heavily upon almost forty years of pastoral experience during which time I have been privileged to know many people who I believe found a greater 'wholeness', often within the limitations of their ongoing illness, and also within the courageous way in which they accepted the reality of death. Some have discovered both healing and cure. Others have been healed but not cured. Whilst a few have been cured but did not find healing in the fullest sense in which it is understood in these pages.

I believe that a combination of good medicine, enlightened counselling and sound religion points the way forward, and that those who are practitioners in all three fields need to work closely together in order to meet the totality of human need.

The devotional Bible readings which follow the subject matter of each chapter are an essential part of the whole exercise. It is hoped that those who use the material in groups will encourage the participants to 'practise' the suggested meditations before they come to the group meeting. I would like to think also that every session will end in a period of quiet waiting upon God. It is in such times that discoveries are made and thoughts and ideas are clarified. Also it is when we pray that our insights become woven into the very stuff of life and being.

Finally I would like to dedicate this small book to my four grandchildren, Thomas, Rachel, Naomi and Daniel, in the hope that as they grow in body, so they will also grow into wholeness.

Howard Booth
May 1985

A NOTE ABOUT THE SUGGESTIONS
FOR GROUP ACTIVITY

There are many different kinds of group activity. Some groups are 'task-centred'; they have a job to do; a sale to organize; a series of worship services to prepare. The leader will try to make sure that the group works effectively and doesn't waste time but moves as smoothly as possible towards the desired goal.

Other groups may be called 'study groups'; they have a subject to investigate; they are going to share their knowledge and resources with each other; such group activity is primarily 'cerebral'; it has more to do with thoughts and ideas than with feelings.

'Therapeutic groups' however are concerned primarily with feelings. They help people to help themselves through mutual support and understanding. They are often organized for people struggling with similar problems — alcoholism, obesity, nervous illness and so on.

There is often a 'spill-over' between the different kinds of groups. A 'task-centred' group may find that one of its members is passing through a difficult personal experience such as a divorce and this may well become apparent and tend to divert the group from its task. A good leader will not ignore the personal needs of one member but will also still try to focus on the aim for which the group is meeting.

Bible study groups often contain people who are interested in the finer points of translation and exegesis but, because the Bible speaks to our deeper human needs, ideas will sometimes give way to feelings as individuals feel that a particular passage is speaking directly to their personal situation.

The suggestions for group activity in this book are designed to promote 'caring and sharing'. There is a 'study' element because material is introduced which some people may not be familiar with, and exploration of the suggested themes with mutual enlightenment is a hopeful possibility. However the aim is to enable individuals and groups to discover an increasing 'wholeness' for themselves. This will happen if members feel free to be themselves and to share their fears and inadequacies as well as their helpful discoveries and renewed strengths.

Those who lead should ask God for the sensitivity to become aware if an individual is under so much strain that private pastoral care is called for. In such cases we should never forget that we have no option but to love one another (John 15:12). The Prior of Taizé puts it in this challenging and stimulating way: 'To have opted for love; that choice opens in a man a wound from which he never recovers'. Those wounds — which have healing properties — come about because we allow ourselves to be vulnerable and we commit ourselves deeply to one another.

There is a risk in participating in 'caring and sharing' groups but there are many rewards. One of the factors which may help this book to be a useful devotional and study guide lies in the suggested Bible passages. If they can be used on the seven days prior to coming to the group meeting they may well provide a foundation upon which effective 'caring and sharing' may take place.

CHAPTER ONE

HEALING FOR OUR DIVIDED SELVES

There is a proper love of self as Jesus in his second great commandment made clear: 'You must love your fellow man *as yourself*' (Matthew 22:39). But this acceptable word needs to be set against another saying: 'If anyone wants to come with me he must *forget himself*, carry his cross and follow me' (Mark 8:34). These two sayings are not contradictory. A proper love of self includes saying no to selfish desires. To love our fellow human beings means that we work creatively for their highest good. To love ourselves means that we work creatively for our own highest good, and self-denial and self-control are essential elements in this process.

If we are to find experiences of inner healing and to move forward towards a greater integration, we should be aware that there is a price to be paid. In Luke 14:28–33 Jesus graphically illustrated what this means. If anyone proposes to build a tower he should first sit down and calculate the cost of it so that he can be sure he has the resources to finish building. If the resources are not available then he would be wiser not to make a start!

This assessment of the real situation will include the painful acknowledgement that within each one of us exists a variety of selves which from time to time struggle with each other. How can we become aware of this?

Are we divided?

Our chapter title presupposes that we are but most of us have only to reflect upon our own inner lives to know that the answer is yes. There is also much confirming evidence from the experience of others:

> 'I am large; I contain a multitude.'   (Walt Whitman)
>
> 'Who am I? This or the other?
> Am I one person today and tomorrow another?
> Am I both at once?'   (Dietrich Bonhoeffer)
>
> 'I don't do what I would like to do; instead I do what I hate.'
>   (St Paul in Romans 7:15)

A convenient way of recognizing our internal divisions which, although painful, can be fun, is to be found in the books by Eric Berne — *Games People*

1

Play (Penguin) — and by Thomas Harris — *I'm OK — You're OK* (Harper & Row USA). The suggestion is that each of us carries around within our own individual selves at least three 'persons' which can be identified as the *Child*, the *Parent* and the *Adult*. The fascinating exercise suggested by both books is that we attempt to discover, by self-observation, which of these three 'selves' emerges in response to a variety of given situations.

The Child is the easiest to distinguish. If we are frustrated from getting our own way we often relapse into childish ways of behaviour: we withdraw co-operation; we indicate that we have felt slighted or hurt; we are asking to be re-accepted, to be loved. Sometimes it works as it did when we were children — but it does nothing for our growth into wholeness!

The Parent is not so easily recognizable but practice can do it. Reflect upon those things you particularly recall or remember about them. Mine for instance were hard-working, industrious and seldom spent any time in leisure activities. Although they have been dead for some years I often seem to hear them say, in the words of John Wesley (himself a workaholic), 'Never be triflingly employed'. Their rather stern moral outlook also obtrudes from time to time and, although with my mind and intellect I have come to accept certain changes in social behaviour as being perfectly acceptable, I sometimes feel distinctly uncomfortable within when I am directly involved in something of which they would not have approved.

The Adult is that self which is able to make more objective appraisals of situations (including an awareness of the 'child' and the 'parent'), and thus to arrive at mature conclusions issuing in responsible actions.

The book by Thomas Harris, whilst using this basic framework, also suggests that there are other selves which cannot be identified within this simple pattern. An illustration of this is to be found in the depths of cruelty to which people can sink in wartime or when their own ultimate safety is threatened. Those who committed unspeakable crimes against humanity in the concentration camps were able to become loving parents and respectable citizens when their social situation was dramatically changed.

Naturally these varied 'selves' cause internal conflicts and when these are particularly acute considerable damage can be done to our inner selves.

The effects of fragmentation

Of course everyone is different and some are far more fortunate in their original parenting than others. Given an awareness of love and having been at the receiving end of expressions of warm affection, we are likely to be better equipped to handle our inner disturbances than those not so fortunate. However, internal divisions occur within each one of us from time to time and their effects may be:

Emotional frustration. Fears which are often irrational; obsessive anxiety; a draining of resources which means that we constantly feel unwell.

Difficulty in forming good relationships. A longing to be able to 'get on' with people but many disappointments. A particular inability to relate to people who are of a similar personality make-up. This may result in our being afraid to commit ourselves to anyone for fear of being hurt. So we withdraw into ourselves and become 'loners'.

Physical symptoms of illness. As the internal conflicts persist so they may produce a chemical imbalance. Endocrinic aberrations release poison into the system, the simplest illustration of which is excessive acidity, causing stomach discomfort and perhaps peptic ulcers. To go to the other extreme there are some doctors like Dr Janet Thompson who, in her book, *Spiritual Considerations in the Prevention, Treatment and Cure of Disease* asserts: 'I am sure that at the root of cancer there is a spiritual trauma; a severe beating of the psychological and physical body of the victim . . . which leads to the development of cancer cells'.

Not every oncologist (cancer specialist) would agree with Dr Thompson but there is a significant body of medical opinion which would direct much more expenditure in cancer research towards more careful investigation of the emotional history of cancer sufferers.

Psychological factors also play a large part in smoking-related diseases and obesity. Smoking is dangerous and a direct cause of illness but millions of people still smoke. Over-eating causes obesity but to control the intake of food and the type of diet we eat is far from easy. Both smoking and over-eating are 'compulsions' which give temporary satisfaction to emotional needs. The best hope of a solution to the problem lies in greater self-understanding. We need to become aware as to why we need to smoke and eat more food than is necessary.

Our divided selves produce stress. We waste emotional energy in futile worries. We push ourselves in order to succeed and to be 'someone'. The result can be a heightening of the blood pressure with its consequent effects upon the cardio-vascular system. An eminent cardiologist, Dr Peter Nixon, now sends some of his patients not to hospital but to a religious community where they can discover inner quiet and be helped to come to terms with themselves.

Possible ways forward

If it is true that the emotional, spiritual and physical factors in healing are closely intertwined, how can we facilitate the movement towards a greater wholeness?

Observation. For many years now I have kept a journal in which I record the more significant events in my life, together with my observations about the way in which I have handled them. On looking back at it I notice that it has often been the difficult situations which I feel that I have handled badly which I have recorded in detail. This is because they have aroused in me an intensity of feeling.

I have become aware that my deepest feelings are aroused when it seems that I am, in some way, being threatened. I am particularly prone to feel badly when I become aware that I am being criticized or that policies which I advocate are being opposed. I note in my journal that I have drawn back from certain actions in which I whole-heartedly believed because I felt my own inner security to have been threatened. I don't enjoy admitting this but it happens to be true.

On the positive side I note from my journal that, over the years, my understanding of these difficult situations has improved. I can laugh at myself much more now than I used to be able to do. Also I have discovered that where tension exists and it is buried under pleasantries, it is better to bring it out into the open — and this has often involved me taking the initiative in dealing with an awkward situation.

When I began to use the parent/child/adult pattern in observation I often found that I was able to identify the different elements as I looked back at my journal. This has helped me especially when I notice that I have become aware of my 'child' and my 'parent' and, having recognized the strength of the feelings they evoke, have nevertheless acted in an 'adult' and responsible manner.

Other people I have known have been helped to express their feelings through art. With a set of paints or crayons they have tried to express how they are feeling on paper. The results have often been weird and wonderful but a trained art-therapist can help them to see 'patterns'. Even without a professional guide, to express oneself through painting or drawing can often be a relief and bring release from tension.

The advantage of a journal is that we can keep referring back to it and try to assess the progress we are making. It becomes a 'tool' for our growth towards a greater wholeness. I suppose that we could also keep our artistic efforts to look back upon, although I have no practical experience of this.

As our ability to cope with ourselves grows and develops so we begin to feel better. We do not waste our emotional energy so easily. We feel less tired and exhausted. This is a direct contribution towards the healing of our divided selves.

Visualization or Mind Control. The phrase 'mind over matter' has passed into common usage. The Bible puts it plainly: 'As a man thinketh in his heart, so he is'. Modern health education posters tell us: 'You are what you eat'. A useful addition to a poster display might be one reading: 'You are what you think'.

At the Bristol Cancer Clinic patients are offered a variety of treatments to help them to cope with their illness and to promote their well-being and wholeness. One of the basic principles taught is that in illness, be it cancer or any other disease or malfunction, you do not just hand yourself over to others and allow them to do with you what they will. You seek all the help and counsel you can get but you remain in control and you expect to play a full part in any decisions taken about your future. This playing an active role involves the deliberate cultivation of positive attitudes of mind, aided by the practices of relaxation and meditation. For those who are committed Christians, this involves the direct use of prayer — both our own personal prayers and the prayer support of others.

Some of the practices suggested at Bristol are based on the work of Dr and Mrs Carl Simonton in the USA. They advocate a combination of traditional therapies (radiotherapy; chemotherapy; surgery) and visualization or mind control techniques. Human beings possess their own immunizing systems. From time to time the victory over cancer is fought and won without the person concerned knowing anything about it at all. What Dr and Mrs Simonton seek to do is to reinforce those natural healing and defensive powers by encouraging their patients to see themselves as getting better and being able to cope. Link this in with the Christian concept of making direct contact with God through prayerful meditation, and you have a powerful addition to the armoury through which you seek a greater wholeness.

Pat Seed died from cancer. When her illness was diagnosed she might — as many do — have relapsed into resignation and self-pity. She didn't but instead set about raising very large sums of money to help in the more accurate diagnosis of cancer. She also sought to live in a positive and meaningful way and this she describes in her book, *One Day at a Time*. The years of life which remained to her were given a quality and meaning which arose directly from her chosen state of mind.

The use of visualization and mind control techniques is not confined to cancer sufferers. In any kind of situation to see yourself as belonging to God who loves you and cares for you and to engage in exercises which remind you that God does care and is concerned for your greater wholeness — this is both sensible and logical.

Take a felt pen and write in large letters on a piece of card: 'IN STILLNESS AND IN BEING QUIET — HERE LIES MY STRENGTH' (based on Isaiah 30:15). Put it in a prominent place and spend time each day finding this inner quiet and putting your divided self directly into God's presence. Then see yourself as becoming more and more whole and less and less divided. Write up the results in your journal and check back from time to time. What happens may seem to take place slowly — but it will be significant.

A CHILDISH KING

Read 1 Kings 21:1–15

Key verse: **Ahab went home, depressed and angry over what Naboth had said to him. He lay down on his bed, facing the wall and would not eat.** (4)

Here is a perfect example of an adult 'child'. Indeed could anything be more typical: going to bed, turning his face to the wall and refusing to eat!

Ahab wanted a piece of land next door to the palace. He was the King and he had not expected Naboth to be so firm in his refusal. But he was a weak king, dominated by his wife, Jezebel (see verse 25). Ahab did not enter into rational discussion with Naboth nor try to see his point of view. He just sulked.

If only Ahab could have stood back from himself and tried to discern the nature of his feelings. Instead he allowed the 'child' to take over and sensible action was impossible. The result was tragedy.

☐ Reflect upon how similar attitudes regularly create havoc in homes, in industry and between nations. If only those concerned would cultivate the art of listening to God, who, if we persist, will help us to become aware of all the conflicting voices which rise from within ourselves and be able to discern the positive from the negative.

☐ Beware however of thinking of these concepts only in relation to others! What about my 'child' within? When was the last occasion on which its emergence spoiled my life and damaged my relationships?

A day in one's life is a small replica of one's own life. If a man does not work on a day in his life, he cannot change his life, and if he says he wishes to work on his life and change it and does not work on a day in his life, his work on himself remains purely imaginary.

(Maurice Nicoll in *Psychological Commentaries*)

THE CONTROLLING SPIRIT

Read Galatians 5:16–26

Key verse: **The Spirit has given us life. He must also control our lives.** (25)

Jesus has come and gone from sight but he lives to guide his people through the Spirit. How fortunate we are and yet how necessary that we should have a guide and comforter, for the struggle is continuous. It is the struggle to decide between alternative courses of action. To decide to follow the 'adult' part of our minds. To seek and somehow lay hold upon 'the mind which was in Christ' (Philippians 2:5). He was — and is — the only truly mature person.

How can this happen? Our key verse gives the clue. We have been given a taste of life. We have 'come alive' in Jesus. This is the work of the Spirit. But the Spirit's work is not now at an end:

> Yet when the work is done,
> The work is but begun. (Charles Wesley)

Edward Wilson of the Antarctic described it in terms of a cog-wheel and a ratchet. Each time the cog-wheel moves up a notch the ratchet slips into place and holds it firm. It does not slip back.

This may sound over-optimistic. In fact we do slip back from time to time. Yes, but if we cultivate the art of being open to the Spirit and building upon the light and knowledge which we have, even if we do sometimes 'backslide', the Spirit will be increasingly in control.

And in the Spirit cry out this one cry: SIN, SIN, SIN, OUT, OUT, OUT! This cry of the heart is better learnt from God by experience than from one man's teaching.

(The Cloud of Unknowing)

SO NEAR AND YET SO FAR

Read Acts 5:1–11

Key verse: **'Ananias, why did you let Satan take control of your heart and make you lie to the Holy Spirit by keeping part of the money you received from the property?'** (3)

Ananias and Sapphira found themselves within a community which was so close that they simply shared everything they had. It was a valid kind of communism. You were not compelled by any discipline to share all your possessions (verse 4); you just did so out of a full heart.

But Ananias and Sapphira were not quite ready. They wanted to belong and felt that they had to demonstrate their total commitment. Therefore they sold their property and gave part to the common purse. But they were divided within themselves. They could not go the whole way. They had to 'hedge their bets' by keeping part of the proceeds back for themselves.

This was perfectly acceptable if it had been done openly. But they wanted to give the impression that they had given all — with tragic results.

If only Ananias and Sapphira had been honest about their reservations, then a different story would have been written. Their mistake was to listen to two conflicting voices and to try to respond to them both.

Jesus said: 'Any town or family which divides itself into groups will fall apart' (Matthew 12:25). So will any person who allows the internal divisions to go on and on, without really attempting to resolve them.

Life is meant to be lived from the centre, a divine Centre. Each one of us can live such a life of amazing power and peace and serenity, of integration and confidence and simplified multiplicity, on one condition — that is if we really want to.

(Thomas R. Kelly, *A Testament of Devotion*)

GROW UP!

Read Ephesians 4:9–16

Key verse: **Instead by speaking the truth in the spirit of love we must grow up in every way to Christ who is the head.** (15)

Our different and conflicting selves never cease to exist. We continue to be jealous, selfish, envious, unloving. The old way was to try and stamp them out — those 'selves' we did not like. The new way is to acknowledge them — even to love them — but to do so because in fact they can be the means whereby we thrust ourselves entirely on the mercy and grace of God knowing that he alone can deal with them.

Children respond easily to pressure; they can be indoctrinated; they can be manipulated. But we do not remain children and we need not remain spiritual children.

Read 1 Corinthians 13:11.

The key to growth lies in our relationship with Jesus who is 'at the still point of the turning world' (T. S. Eliot).

Every organization requires a head whose job it is to hold all the different parts and functions together; to deal with the factions which do exist; to give purpose, thrust and meaning so that the organization can operate effectively.

Jesus is our 'head' and we have the responsibility of referring our conflicting selves to him. I once heard a saintly minister say that when he was faced with several possible alternative courses of action, he spent time quietly, before God, going along each of the different ways in his imagination. Usually along one of these ways he felt a sense of peace. That was the way to go.

> *To be a Christian*
> *is to bind oneself to Christ,*
> *but to the total Christ,*
> *head and body,*
> *in order to live consciously, every day,*
> *that mystery of love*
> *which is the historical realization*
> *of the eternal plan of the Father.*
> (Michel Quoist)

CREATIVE IMAGINATION

Read Psalm 121

Key verse: **He will protect you as you come and go, now and for ever.** (8)

Use this Psalm to visualize the nature of the God who loves you.

Life is a series of comings and goings, of little deaths and little resurrections. We are born and we die but in between these two significant events we are up and down, confident and depressed, loving and hating, living in trust and living in fear. The Psalm assures us that God is with us in all these experiences.

Creator. Visualize a familiar mountain. Recall its solidity, strength and endurability.

Helper. Now you feel yourself falling; your 'divisions' are showing. You are 'coming apart at the seams'. When this happens — look up — he will not let you fall. He will hold you together.

Sustainer. Amid 'all the changing scenes of life' he supplies strength according to the needs of the hour (see 1 Corinthians 1:8).

A minister's wife once had the courage to write to a Christian weekly to say how her false understanding of God's true nature had brought her to the point of breakdown. She resented the 'god' who took her husband away from her for so many long hours and interfered with their family life. Now she had found someone who had helped her to discover the true God who really loved her. Her last sentence in the letter was: 'Now I have become a real person'.

Use your imagination with other biblical 'images' like the one given in this Psalm. Ask God to bring them alive in your imagination. He will!

> *The mystery of our temporal and eternal destiny*
> *is disclosed to us only in the great textbook of God —*
> *the word in which he speaks to us*
> *and tells us who he is.*
>
> (Helmut Thielicke)

DESIRE FOR LIFE

Read John 5:1–9
Key verse: **'Do you want to get well?'** (6)

Adequate motivation is of prime importance in recovery from illness. From time to time in my work as a hospital chaplain a doctor or nurse has said to me: 'Can you help so-and-so? They seem to have lost the will to live. There is no good medical reason why they should not get well again'.

Jesus may have felt that this man's illness was in fact acting as a shield. It had become his guarantee of an easy living. People evidently carried him about and fed him. If he was fit again he would have to fend for himself — and he hadn't done this for 38 years!

In a perverse kind of way it is possible to enjoy being ill. It can be a protection from facing up to the challenge of responsible living. I have known elderly parents who have made their single daughter's life a misery by using their sickness to 'enslave' her.

Now use this passage as the basis for a devotional meditation:

First — be still.

See the pool — cool — inviting — but you cannot get in.

Now Jesus is here and he is probing your motivation. He says to you as he said to the man in the story so long ago: 'Do you want to get well?'

Remember, you cannot fool Jesus. He knows all about your 'soggy' centre.

Now his hands are upon you (feel them).

His 'wholeness' is seeping through your entire being.

Already you are feeling better. Give him thanks.

> *We are invited and summoned*
> *to take seriously*
> *the victory of God's glory*
> *in this man Jesus*
> *and to be joyful in him.*
> *That we may live in thankfulness,*
> *and not in fear.*
> (Karl Barth)

TUNNEL VISION

Read Hebrews 12:1–6
Key verse: **Let us keep our eyes fixed on Jesus, on whom our faith depends from beginning to end.** (2)

First glance back at Hebrews 11. This is the record of the 'great cloud of witnesses' who survived and won through by virtue of their faith and trust.

☐ You belong to such a community (verse 1). Your roots go back to Hebrews 11 and even before then. The community of Christian love exists today. You can discover such a group of God's people if you have not already done so. You also can 'care and share'.

☐ Don't allow discouragement to make you give up (verse 3). If and when you are tempted to do so, look towards Jesus. His endurance is your guarantee of renewal.

☐ Always pay particular attention to what is happening to you when the going is rough (verse 5). We bring punishment upon ourselves and we suffer from the consequences of our mistakes. This is life!

☐ Reflect on this sentence written by Dr Martin Israel: 'I personally do not doubt that God wills wholeness for all his creatures, but that disease and suffering are sometimes necessary for wholeness to be attained' (*Healing as Sacrament*). On the surface this is a hard saying. Is it true?

> *How does God speak to us?*
> *He speaks to us through our past.*
> *He speaks to us through our present situation.*
> *And he speaks to us through our own arguments,*
> *through our fears and failures,*
> *through his love,*
> *through other people,*
> *books,*
> *pain and suffering.*
> *He speaks to us by every possible means*
> *at every possible time.*
> (Rosalind Rinker)

HEALING FOR OUR DIVIDED SELVES

Suggestions for group work

1. Read Romans 7:21–25. Here Paul describes his own inward struggle. Do you recognize anything similar within your own experience? Go round the group and say if you identify with what Paul has written here and, if so, how? (Let anyone pass who doesn't feel able to respond.) What happened to Paul between Romans 7 and 8? (See the opening verses of chapter 8.)

2. Discuss the difference between a discussion group and a 'caring and sharing group'. What kind of group do you think yours is intended to be? Share your expectations.

3. Compare the following scripture verses and ask yourselves if they have anything specific to say to you as a group and as individuals:
   'What he thinks is what he really is.' (Proverbs 23:7)
   'Examine me, O God, and know my mind; test me and discover my thoughts. Find out if there is any evil way in me and guide me in the everlasting way.' (Psalm 139:23–24)
   '. . . we take every thought captive and make it obey Christ.' (2 Corinthians 10:5)
Do you attempt to control your thought life, and if so, how?

4. Prepare two posters to put up in your church porch. The first one begins TO BE HEALTHY IS . . . The second one begins HEALING IS . . . Complete the sentences and remember that the posters are intended to catch the eye and make people think. Consider actually putting the posters up!

CHAPTER TWO

HEALING THROUGH DEEPER UNDERSTANDING

In the last chapter we saw how damaging to our health our internal divisions can be and we began to look for practical ways of discovering a greater 'wholeness'. Now we go one stage further. Our internal divisions can actually be the means whereby we discover renewed health and vitality, providing we can understand something about what is happening to us, and how deeply inlaid thought-patterns can spoil our purposeful existence.

Darkness and dawn

Dark moments come to all of us. Depression can be an illness if it pervades all our lives and seems to stay with us for an eternity. But who has not been depressed? Perhaps it has happened because we have felt slighted; our true worth has not been appreciated. Life has not turned out as we hoped it would; we have been let down, deserted, the future is bleak. This may be the very time God can use to help us get into touch with reality. The Book of Ecclesiasticus asks a question we might well ask of ourselves: 'Who will speak up for a man who is his own enemy, or respect one who disparages himself?' (Ecclesiasticus 10:29).

When we are 'down' is the best time to set this process going. The previous verse to the one already quoted from Ecclesiasticus can help us: 'My son, in all modesty keep your self-respect and value yourself at your true worth' (10:28). When we are 'living on a high note', when we are riding 'on the crest of a wave', this may not be the best time to get a true and accurate picture of ourselves. But when the night seems black 'and even the stars are hidden', such times can provide good material out of which to fashion change.

We begin our search for a more worthwhile self-evaluation by asking ourselves why it is that we *feel* as we do in these dark moments. Of course external events will play some part. Circumstances have changed in such ways as we did not want to happen and we feel unsure, even afraid. But the nature of our response to the challenge will depend upon what we are as persons. Our feelings about the situation are more important than the events themselves and will determine our attitude towards our 'dark night of the soul'. How can we get into touch with our feelings in such ways as will enable us to change those destructive thought-patterns which can adversely affect both our happiness and our health?

Use other people as mirrors in which we see ourselves

I can think of a number of people of whom I have been critical. Often I have kept my thoughts about them to myself but sometimes I have voiced them to my wife or to a friend. Indeed the person of whom I am critical may well be a friend; one whom I visit frequently and who visits me. There are many things about them which I like — but I do not feel sure about them. I sometimes question their loyalty to me.

I had often read the passage in Matthew 7:1–5 which includes the words: 'Judge not that you be not judged . . . Why do you see the speck that is in your brother's eye but do not notice the log which is in your own eye? You hypocrite . . .' I had used those words in sermons and in writing, but I can recall the day when they came alive for me within an actual relationship situation. When I realized that in fact the person concerned highlighted my own insecurity. Then the important matter I had to deal with first of all concerned me. My own thought-patterns had to be examined. It was a searching process but eventually it brought insight and enlightenment — and I certainly *felt* a good deal better.

The truth is that we often project our own faults on to others. The desire to do this will always be with us; we do not easily escape from our human frailty. But the actual realization that this is so can transform our understanding. It can mean a more sober and accurate self-picture; and what is even more important — we shall not allow our negative feelings about someone to erupt into destructive actions. We shall say quietly to ourselves: 'There, but for the grace of God, go I. . . . What can I do to help this person who, without knowing it, has given me insight into my true self?'

Think carefully about what our critics say about us

We all have our critics and eventually, what they have to say comes back to us. Of course we resent it and are angry. The natural reaction is to hit back and give as good as we get! In fact the initial anger may be quite a healthy sign providing that we don't allow it to drive common-sense out of the window. What our critics say about us may provide material for careful reflection.

I recall that once it was suggested to me that I undertake a standard psychological test. I had to answer a very long series of questions and give some indication of what I thought about myself in a wide variety of circumstances and situations. Then I received a written analysis and was told to go away and quietly reflect upon what it said.

That assessment provided me with much material both for thought and prayer. I can still recall the hurt feelings which erupted during the time I spent considering what had been given to me. Those same feelings still come back from time to time, and immediately I am transported back in memory to the incidents which first gave rise to them. Such increased ability as I have to deal with them goes back to that salutary time in my life when I first became aware of them.

Take the initiative in improving relationships

When I was a young minister an incident happened to me the significance of which I did not really appreciate at that time. I had just gone to a new appointment full of ideas and enthusiasm and tried to make all kinds of changes before I had secured the confidence and trust of the people. One man who had belonged to that church all his life said very little to me either by way of criticism or encouragement until eventually he went into hospital for an extended spell and I visited him every week. Towards the end of that time he felt able to say to me something like this: 'When you came to be our minister I wasn't drawn to you. You seemed to be so full of your own importance. But even if I didn't like you I was determined to love you and I don't really know whether you have changed or I have, but I have come to care for you a great deal'. Looking back over the years I can see now that we had both changed, but that his attitude towards me was the significant factor in bringing about a new and improved situation.

Look for the best in people and identify what you can really appreciate — then express your appreciation. Don't be insincere about what you say — that will soon be detected. But if you are genuinely appreciative of someone's words or actions — then encourage them by sharing your thoughts and feelings with them.

Often where there has been a breakdown in relationships some kind of initiative is called for. If someone does not make a move the wounds will fester and the situation deteriorate.

The late Dr Edwin Sangster was known and loved by thousands of people — but a few were jealous and tried to erect barriers around him and minimize his growing influence. One Christmas he was writing out his cards and was addressing one to a critic who had played a leading role in the efforts 'to put him in his place'. A friend who was staying with him ventured to comment: 'I see you are sending a card to so-and-so. Don't you remember what he tried to do to you?' 'Yes, I do remember', the good Doctor replied, 'but I've remembered to forget'.

Sometimes a genuine admission of your own part in a breakdown will cause the dam to burst and the tears to flow. But after the tears can come the laughter. After the sorrow, the joy. Darkness is always the prelude to the dawn.

Understand more about ourselves through our illnesses

Can our illnesses be educational experiences? Dr Patrick Pietroni was recently appointed the first Chairman of a new organization entitled 'The British Association for Holistic Medicine'. Soon afterwards he gave a lecture to the British Association for the Advancement of Science in which he pleaded for a new kind of patient-doctor relationship: 'The traditional hierarchical structure of this relationship needs to be finally put to rest . . . Doctors are viewed as fighting the disease and all too often this involves fighting the patient . . . It is better to know what sort of patient has the disease than what sort of disease the patient has'.

When Dr Pietroni sees a patient he often draws a small circle in which he inserts a shaded slice. The slice represents the symptoms which have been presented; the rest of the circle the whole person. He suggests to the patient that the symptoms presented may be saying something both to him and to them about their deeper needs and about how this may have been affecting their chosen life-style. He sees the doctor-patient relationship as providing opportunity for new discoveries, new insights — and consequently a co-operative way of tackling the problem(s) in which both the doctor and the patient have a responsible part to play. Drugs may or may not be necessary. A more disciplined life-style including meditation and relaxation practices may bring blood pressure down to acceptable levels without recourse to beta-blockers (an anti-hypertensive drug).

Today many of the 'diseases of civilization' cannot be cured by 'magic bullets' in the shape of ever more powerful drugs, or even by high technology, advanced and sophisticated as it is. Heart attacks, diseases of the cerebral-vascular system, nervous illness including depression, all need a combination of medical skills and psychological insights. Behind many of the destructive habits such as smoking, over-eating, excessive drinking, unhealthy sexual practices, there often exist dissatisfied people who are snatching at excitement in these ways in order to mask their boredom with life. Such people need a reason for living, or to put it in another way, they need to acquire new motivation and more substantial inner resources. It is these spiritual blessings which vital religious faith can supply.

Some years ago a friend of mine went to visit a church for a week-end preaching engagement. He was entertained by a delightful hostess but only saw his host briefly at mealtimes because he had pressing business matters to attend to over the whole week-end. Nevertheless he seemed to enjoy my friend's company in the brief time they spent together. Some weeks afterwards my friend had an urgent telephone call. Was it possible for him to return to this home particularly to see the husband who had completely broken down in health? He went and established a relationship with the man who was driven by tremendous inner compulsions towards success. The sad thing was that he was indeed already successful, but he had become the kind of person who must always be going further. He could not stand still and he could not be still.

Between them (and with the help and support of the man's wife) they worked out a new style of life and new work-patterns. He discovered a better reason for living; learnt how to trust other people and to delegate — and that there are more important things in life than making money. Years afterwards my friend received a letter from that man in which he said: 'I am so glad that I had that breakdown; without it I would never have made the discoveries which have transformed my life'.

Discover new ways to acquire deeper resources

This also is an adventure in understanding. Many of the disabilities we acquire through unhealthy ways of living or through unfortunate circumstances, remain with us all our lives. The challenge is in the way we deal with them. A young man named Alan came to visit a conference arranged by the Churches' Council for Health and Healing. He was a spastic and when he began to speak his faltering voice and jerky movements made many of us feel distinctly uncomfortable. But he got through to us. He described how a fundamental change had taken place in his life. How caring people had helped him to discover the relevance of Jesus for his own life and so his attitude had been changed. Previously he had bitterly resented his disability; now he had come to accept it and was determined to live as full a life as possible within his limitations. Especially he wanted to help others with similar burdens.

Afterwards in group discussion someone raised the question of 'normality'. Was the new Alan 'normal' and we, who did not have to carry his recognizable disability, the 'abnormal' ones? Certainly compared with many of us, in his attitudes and through the resources he had discovered, Alan was truly 'healthy'.

Then the conversation turned to our own disabilities. They were not all to be seen on the surface but many of us struggled with our own inadequacies, our difficulties in making relationships, our lack of confidence in ourselves, our deep psychological wounds. When this intimacy had been established and we trusted one another, we were able to go on to say how these 'wounds' were still with us, but in a variety of ways we had discovered how to cope. For most of us our 'wounds' were still very much part of our lives and had enabled us to help both ourselves and others. We had become 'wounded healers'.

The therapeutic value of our inward discoveries is wide and far-reaching. Once this kind of journey has begun it can go on. Indeed it can become an exciting game which you enjoy playing. But it is not morbid. It is not a miserable process of introspection. It is an adventure into territory previously ignored which can now become the source of new life and hope. We are healed through our greater understanding. We grow into greater wholeness by working away at the insights we gain from our 'inwardness'.

LIVING WATER

Read John 4:5–26

Key verse: **'Whoever drinks the water that I will give him will never be thirsty again. The water that I will give him will become a spring which will provide him with living water and give him eternal life.'** (14)

The possibility of a never-ending supply of fresh water excited the woman who spent so much time in carrying water, often over considerable distances. Wells were not to be found everywhere. It took a little time to sink in that this strange and commanding person was talking about something quite different. Something which involved her and the way of life she had been living. This 'living water' could only be hers if she made an exciting discovery which would involve her in drastic changes in her way of life.

We are not told if these drastic changes ever took place. She was however deeply impressed by Jesus because immediately she got back to town she told everybody about her experience. She had been made to ask some deep and probing questions about herself, and she must have wondered what the eventual outcome would be.

☐ Spend time putting yourself in this woman's place. Hear, as she heard, about the possibility of being able to tap a deep well of inward resources which will never dry up; never be exhausted. Visualize that well. See it bubbling and dancing with supplies of clear, fresh water from an underground spring.

☐ Then ask God to show you what rubble in your life is blocking this supply and preventing it rising as it should and could, within yourself. Remember that the very force of this stream of life is trying to get rid of the blockage. He (the author of life and giver of living water) is on your side. As you co-operate with him all kinds of things can happen.

Isaac dug again the wells which had been dug during the time of Abraham and which the Philistines had stopped up after Abraham's death (Genesis 26:18). *Should you be doing the same?*

INWARD LOOK

Read Galatians 6:1–5

Key verse: **And keep an eye on yourself, so that you will not be tempted too.** (1)

The key verse represents almost an aside — but it is pregnant with meaning.

One of John Wesley's helpers was a barber in Leeds by the name of William Shent. He had been a pioneer of the work in that city and had welcomed John Wesley when he first preached there. He had been persecuted for his endeavours and had suffered a great deal of hardship.

Now he had become a 'backslider'. He had 'fallen from grace'. In Mr Wesley's absence, and without more ado, his fellow preachers had turned him out. They had 'excommunicated' him.

When he heard about it John Wesley was indignant and, on his next visit to Leeds, castigated the preachers who had taken this severe action. 'O brethren', he cried, 'tell it not in Gath. Where is your gratitude? Where is your compassion? Where is your Christianity? Let us set him on his feet once more'.

What the preachers had failed to do was to 'keep an eye on themselves'. If they had looked into their own hearts they might have acted differently.

Charles Wesley expressed a similar thought in this way:
> *Let me cast myself aside,*
> *All that feeds my knowing pride,*
> *Not to man, but God submit,*
> *Cast my reasoning at his feet.*

When we are tempted to justify our harsh criticisms of others — stop — take an inward glance. It may save a thousand regrets.

PRISON PRAISE

Read Philippians 1:12–26

Key verse: **I want you to know, my brothers, that the things which have happened to me have really helped the progress of the gospel.**   (12)

Some years ago I found myself in a place where I didn't particularly want to be. Many of the satisfactions and supports I had known elsewhere were now denied me. I felt lonely and unappreciated. One day I took the whole matter to God in my time of private prayer and I received a direct answer: 'You have lived too long with the support of a variety of different "props". Now you are thrust more upon your own resources. This experience will either make or break you'.

I am glad now that it happened. I discovered something I didn't know about myself and I discovered new insights into the nature of God.

Paul seems to have spent a good deal of time in prison. At times it must have seemed a dreadful waste. He could have been out and about among the people. He could have been telling the good news. Instead he was confined within the walls of a prison. What on earth was God up to? This passage makes clear just how Paul's faith and trust triumphed over circumstances.

☐   Members of the Praetorian Guard heard the good news. As each day he spoke to different guards so he was able to answer their questions. And they did not keep their conversations with Paul to themselves. They told others. Soon the whole Praetorian Guard knew the reasons why Paul was in prison.

☐   The local church was enlivened by his example and became much more effective in proclaiming Christ. True, some of them saw the situation as an opportunity to proclaim their own particular understanding of Christ which was different from Paul's. But he was even happy about this (verse 18). The fact that they had been stirred to action at all was cause for rejoicing. He would leave the ultimate issues with God.

Reflect on this verse written by Kathleen Raine:

I am the part that I must play,   *Of good and evil, time and place,*
I am the journey I must go,   *Before the story all is told.*
All that I am I must endure   *All that is possible must be*
And bear the burden of my years   *Before the concord can be full*
                                          Of earth's great cry of joy and woe.

CREATIVE RELATIONSHIPS

Read James 3:1–12
Key verse: **Just think how large a forest can be set on fire by a tiny flame!
And the tongue is like a fire . . .**   (5–6)

I was on holiday in Scotland and on Sunday heard the Church of Scotland
minister tell a story about a boy called John Angus. A new fire extinguisher
had been delivered to the school and John Angus arrived early one morning
before any of the teachers had arrived. The minister, who lived opposite to
the school, had an emergency call from another of the children who said,
'John Angus wants to know how to turn the water off'. On going over to the
school he found John Angus saturated with water and with his finger over the
nozzle of the extinguisher, trying desperately to keep the water inside — but
with little success. The moral was then rubbed in forcibly: 'Never start what
you cannot stop!'

The means by which we cultivate our relationships largely depend upon
words. There are other ways of communicating and a discerning observer
can sometimes see by our expressions (our body language) that we do not
always mean the words we say. But words are the vehicle which we use
generally to cultivate our relationships with one another.

☐   *'Do not use harmful words in talking'* (Ephesians 4:29). It is a regular
temptation to talk about other people and to encourage others to do the same
— and to be critical and destructive about them. Ask the Holy Spirit to
remind you to shut up! And encourage others to do the same.

☐   *'Use only helpful words — the kind that will build up and provide what is needed'*
(Ephesians 4:29). Some American textbooks of popular psychology use the
phrase 'positive strokes'. It is amazing what good can be achieved by honest
words of encouragement, genuinely spoken. If we do harm by some of the
words we utter, we also have an adverse effect upon others by the words we
keep locked up inside us which, if spoken, would bring new hope and added
strength. Be a Barnabas — a son of encouragement.

Think over these words by Catherine de Hueck Doherty:

*The essence of prayer is to hear the voice of another, of Christ, but likewise to hear the
voice of each person I meet in whom Christ also addresses me. His voice comes to me in
every human voice, and his face is infinitely varied . . . Perfect prayer seeks this presence of
Christ and recognizes it in every human face.*

SITUATION ETHICS

Read John 8:2–11

Key verse: **As they stood there asking him questions he straightened up and said to them: 'Whichever of you has committed no sin may throw the first stone at her'.** (7)

It is a simple fact of pastoral experience that those who most readily condemn others seem to have little love in their hearts. It also seems to be true that those who hold tight and rigid views on doctrinal matters or on church order, seldom seem really to listen to what other people say. Could it be that they are so insecure within themselves that to allow their beliefs to be challenged is far too threatening?

The first thought which arises from this passage is that although two people had been engaged in an adulterous act, it was the woman who was arrested and charged. This reflects the differing status of women in Bible times. The situation has changed, but many would say that it has not changed enough.

The second thought is that Jesus seems to have been way ahead of his time in his moral judgements. If ever there was a case of 'situation ethics', this was it. Jesus used the incident to make the hearers think about their own actions. If hearts had been truly opened those who disappeared would have had some lurid stories to tell.

But although Jesus did not condemn the woman he did not condone her actions. His final word to her was to make the best use of this new and unexpected opportunity by ceasing to sacrifice her womanhood so easily.

— *Each time you are tempted to pour out hot words of condemnation, ask if you really know enough about the person or persons concerned. Are you aware of their particular problems and social circumstances?*

— *Remember the Indian Prayer: 'Great Spirit — grant that I may not criticize my neighbour until I have walked a mile in his moccasins'.*

KNOWN, LED AND FED

Read John 10:1–10

Key verse: **'When he has brought them out, he goes ahead of them, and the sheep follow him, because they know his voice.'** (4)

We all like to feel that we are known. A helpful relationship is often established because we feel that the other person understands us; knows the kind of people we are.

Remember this — Jesus 'knows' you far better than even your closest friends. He understands the different pressures that have shaped and are shaping your life. When you feel rebellious and complaining, recall the lines of a simple chorus:

> Jesus knows all about your troubles;
>
> He will guide till the day is through.

The sheepfold is a good place to be in for a while but it is not a 'hidey hole'; it is a place of preparation. The time comes when we are led out into the world of sin, failure, temptation, warped ambitions — which is the real world which you and I know so well.

But he does not drive us out and stay behind himself. He goes ahead and before us. There is no experience we shall be called upon to face which he has not known. He is the pioneer — the fore-runner (see Hebrews 12:2–3).

It is by being outside that we shall 'become'. If the danger is outside the sheepfold, so is the pasture — the food which we need to sustain us and which enables our continued growth.

My friends in the Grail Community have a poster which says: 'To help one person to grow is to help to build the world'. This is precisely what Jesus does for us — then invites us to share with him in the adventure of leading and helping others. Read through Philippians 2:1–12 — and be thankful.

I CAN'T — WE CAN

Read Matthew 11:28–30
Key verse: **'The yoke I will give you is easy, and the load I will put on is light.'**   (30)

Meaningful living includes the acceptance of responsibility. We all have to carry our 'loads'; there is no escaping taking on our proper share. Anyway we shall be the poorer if we try to foist off our proper burdens on to others.

The purpose of the yoke, however, is to make the job easier. It has been made by a master craftsman and it fits snugly and securely. It helps to take the strain.

Better still — we are in double harness. We are 'yoked' with Jesus. He helps us by initiating us into the best ways of moving forward with our portion of the load. We may not feel that it is light, but it is certainly lighter than it would be without the support and strength of our partner.

I was talking with someone about a mutual friend who had tackled a difficult job with great courage and considerable success. 'He was made for the job', I said. 'Not so', my friend replied, 'in fact it was the job which made him. Prior to taking this on he tended to amble through life. This appointment stretched him for the first time'.

Later I told my friend what the other person had said about him. He smiled and said: 'Little did he know how desperate I became at one stage and how near I was to giving up. Then one day I said to God, "I can't do it — but *we* can"'.

Read 2 Corinthians 12:9–10.

Tabulate in your mind your own special areas of weakness.

Think of incidents when you have become conscious that you were in receipt of added resources.

In what ways can our weaknesses become our strengths?

Pray this vital passage in to the deep inward areas of your being.

HEALING THROUGH DEEPER UNDERSTANDING
Suggestions for group work

1. You may have reacted adversely to some of the suggestions made in this chapter and queried their wisdom. You may even feel that the suggestions seem to encourage unhealthy introspection. If you do feel like this then say so. What did you feel about the Bible readings? Share your various responses and be prepared to query your own initial reactions.

2. Sociologists point out that churches sited in different areas often seem to reflect the general views of those who live around them; e.g., suburban middle-class churches are attended by people who vote Conservative or SDP and who read the *Guardian*, the *Times* or the *Telegraph*. The implication is that the nature of faith is moulded by its social environment rather than the other way round. Is this true? Should it be so?

3. Can you illustrate some of the suggestions made in this chapter from your own practical experience? Could you share the incidents with each other, being careful not to break confidences or to talk about people known to you all who are not present?

4. The idea that illness can be an educational experience is difficult for some people to swallow! How do you all feel about it? Any personal insights you can share from your own experiences of illness?

CHAPTER THREE

HEALING THROUGH SUFFERING

The title of this chapter may seem to convey a contradiction of ideas. Healing is often understood to be taking place when suffering is eliminated . . . Many people involved in the healing professions would say that their aim is to relieve suffering or to help people to avoid it or escape from it.

Jesus of course suffered — but he was different! He had a unique mission which included suffering on behalf of others. His purpose in life was redemptive and this involved him in rejection, hardship, physical, mental and spiritual pain. The Bible however, whilst being clear about the uniqueness of Jesus, seems to suggest that (a) suffering was necessary to his development towards perfection (see Hebrews 2:9–10) and (b) that his disciples are called upon to share his sufferings (see 1 Peter 2:21 and Mark 8:34–35). In St Matthew's Gospel alone there are some 200 verses which are about suffering. If the gospel is about healing, it is also about suffering.

Should suffering be welcomed?

No one wants to suffer. Jesus himself would have welcomed a way out of the agonies of the Garden of Gethsemane (Mark 14:36). But if suffering is not to be sought, it is not always wise to avoid it. Physical pain is often a pointer to something which is wrong; our 'balance' has been upset; we are 'out of gear'; if we simply remove the pain by masking the symptoms with drugs, we may fail to get at the real source of the trouble, and our latter state may be worse than our first.

Suffering should not be embraced nor should it be passively accepted. Often it is a challenge to us to summon up all our own resources and seek all the help we can from others so that our suffering can be fought, resisted and overcome. If we just deny it or sit down under it we may fail to discover what our suffering is saying to us.

A man I knew years ago refused to accept that his wife had ceased to love him. Courageously she had told him that their marriage was a mistake. She had not been unfaithful but she wanted to break their relationship and begin her life again. He wouldn't hear of it. He would not allow her even to speak of it. He totally refused to explore with her the reasons why they had come to this point in their lives. He showered her with gifts and attention and lived out a charade by playing the part of a happily married husband — but it was make-believe. It could not carry on. Reality had to be faced and one day he came home to find her gone. Even then he would not acknowledge the truth and told his friends that she had gone away for a while and would soon be back. In the end the suffering which came to him because of his refusal to face up to the situation honestly was infinitely worse. As a person he just disintegrated. It was awful to see him wallowing in self-pity.

If only he had allowed the pain to speak to him. If only he had asked serious questions about why their marriage had failed. It might in fact have been saved. But he deluded himself and paid a terrible price.

A different story

Out of a very different situation Frances Young has told how she and her husband Bob faced the limitations placed upon their lives when their first-born son, Arthur, was discovered to be very severely handicapped. This is a challenge which, as she acknowledges, many other couples have had to face. Frances, however, is a theologian who feels that she has been called to bridge the gap between academic theology and the Christian experience of those who occupy the pews in our churches. She is also now ordained and, as a Christian minister, is seen as one who has 'the cure of souls'.

Her book is called *Face to Face* (Epworth Press 1985) and in it she has been prepared to reveal not only the practical and personal difficulties they have encountered as a family (she and Bob have two other children), but also her own vulnerability as she has wrestled with the deepest questioning of the human spirit. Frances has plumbed the depths of despair; she has faced up to that awful question 'Why?' time and time again. She has rebelled as she has contemplated how different life could have been if Arthur had been 'normal'. She also wonders about Arthur's future. What will happen to him if he outlives his parents? Will the day come when he has to go into an institution?

She has not discovered any easy answers to her questions — but she has found help in the realism of the Psalms; the experience of Job — and in her contemplations on the cross of Christ. The Psalms echo her own 'ups and downs' and have been the vehicle whereby she has been able to be honest with God. The Book of Job clearly states the problem of human suffering and rejects the answers given by Job's 'comforters', namely that his suffering is in direct proportion to his sin. The answer given in the book is not really an answer at all. It just puts the question against a different background. Job sees the wonder and majesty and glory of God — and as Frances suggests — 'In God's presence the demand for explanation ceases. God is sufficient in himself to bring a perspective which transcends and transforms'.

In the cross of Christ that 'presence' is earthed in the deepest and profoundest of ways. Jesus enters directly in to every experience of darkness and desolation — 'My God, my God, why hast thou forsaken me?' — but even there is not lost or defeated. He is able finally to say, 'Into thy hands I commend my spirit'. To quote Frances again: 'The absence of God and the presence of God. The agony of the world and the joy of the Kingdom. The one does not do away with the other, but it does transform it'.

She is able to express many of the deepest feelings and experiences she has known in moving and sensitive poetry and ends one poem in this way:

> 'How can I tell how much I hope in you?
> You'll be what you will be.
> How can I speak the trust I place in you?
> You are my eternity'.

What does it mean to be 'a whole person'?

Obviously there is much more to 'wholeness' than what often appears on the surface. A person may be vibrantly healthy — strong and active and with no need of the assistance of doctor, psychotherapist or counsellor. Such a person is in control of events and leads a 'normal' life. They function competently and are recognized as able and indeed gifted. They often occupy positions of leadership in society.

What do they lack? They appear to be fair, honest and just. They play their part in human affairs and indeed are pillars of society and may well be active in their local church. Is it possible that their 'wholeness' is affected by their lack of compassion? On a poster somewhere I saw the following quotation: 'No man is whole unless he is joined to the sufferings of others'. This reminded me of a person I met in a conference in which I once shared on the subject of 'Health and Healing'. After a number of sessions in which a measure of confidence and trust had been established, she began to share her experience of deep depression. For years she had been ill in the clinical sense and had been to a number of doctors and therapists seeking help. Now she told us how she had found someone who she felt was going to be of real help to her. This was how she explained what had happened to her:

'Many of the people to whom I have been for help have seemed to be detached and have dealt with me in what they call a "professional" way. They have also seemed to be concerned to help me because that was their job and they wanted to be seen as people who were good at it. This man doesn't seem to worry about his reputation. He doesn't appear to want to do me good. He is just content to be with me and feel his way into my pain. At last I feel that I have found someone who understands and for me it is a real glimmer of light at the end of a very long tunnel.'

Compassion

Three teachers of pastoral theology got together in the USA to write a book about Compassion. It arose out of conversations they had held together over several years. As they wrote they were acutely conscious of their own comfortable backgrounds and life-styles. Many of the agonies of people in different parts of the world passed them by. They knew about them but had not experienced any of them at first hand. Eventually 'a man emerged from the hazy background of our ambiguous feelings and presented himself to us as a representative of the world which seemed to accuse us'. That man was a Paraguayan doctor named Joel Filartiga. With his equally dedicated wife he cares for poor people in a small town two hours away from the capital city of Asuncion. But he is not only a medical doctor; he is also a leader of the poor in the fight against cruelty and oppression. As he listens to them as they recount their stories, he picks up his pencils and draws, for he is a fine artist and can somehow express what they are feeling through his pictures.

One day the authorities decided to get at him through his son. So on March 30th 1976 they kidnapped seventeen-year-old Joelito and tortured him to death. But their sorrow and grief did not drive Joel and Nidia into seclusion. Instead they laid out their son's distorted and bloodstained body exactly as it had been found. Thus they made their protest — but at what a cost!

Later the powerful drawings of Joel Filartiga were included in the book on Compassion written by the teachers of pastoral theology. As they themselves say, 'the drawings in this book may prove to be more important than the words'. (See *Compassion* by Nouven, McNeill and Morrison, published by Darton, Longman and Todd.)

Loving and being loved

To find a healing which promotes a greater wholeness of body, mind and spirit can only come when we realize that we are loved and that we are capable of loving. The first Epistle of John makes this abundantly clear. We are privileged to know what love is because 'Christ gave his life for us'. The only proper response is 'to give our lives for our brothers' (1 John 3:16). 'Our love should not just be words and talk; it must be true love which shows itself in action' (1 John 3:18).

I myself experienced a healing of the Spirit, when many years ago I found myself, almost by accident, in Chester Cathedral, on the eve of beginning what was for me a new and difficult job. Suddenly it came to me in a way I had never realized before. God was saying to me, 'Don't worry about it. I'm with you. I'm on your side'. I have known many times of bewilderment and depression since those far off days but I have never lost the sense of knowing that I am loved.

In my wide margined Bible I have written a brief note at the side of the 1 John passage. It simply says, 'But to love is not easy!' Indeed it is not. It often requires an exercise of the will and calls for strong self-discipline. But there is no healing or growing wholeness without love — both received and given.

In summary

It may be helpful to set out what we have been attempting to say in the form of three statements:

1. Suffering is not to be sought (save when we know it will follow from doing right); the reasons for it are often hidden — but it can be used when it is offered to God.

2. Through suffering we can make discoveries about life's true meaning and so our real health is improved and we find healing at the deepest of levels.

3. Suffering can actually be a means of healing because it can point us to the values which really matter and which will endure when all else has failed — simplicity, acceptance (in the best sense) and love.

THE SPIRIT AS ADVOCATE

Read Romans 8:18–27

Key verse: **And God who sees into the hearts of men, knows what the thought of the Spirit is; because the Spirit pleads with God on behalf of his people and in accordance with his will.** (27)

Kitty Muggeridge was desperately ill. Her husband and family were at her bedside. She had two visions. The first was that heaven's door was opening. The second was that her husband's blood was dripping into her veins. His life was being given to her because he loved her so. Heaven's door was then closed and, almost reluctantly, she returned to earth. (See *Gazing on Truth,* Triangle SPCK.)

When C. S. Lewis was with his wife as she lay near to death, he asked her 'If it is allowed' if she would come to him on his death bed. 'Allowed', she said, 'Heaven would have a job to hold me, and as for Hell, I'd break it into bits'. (See *A Grief Observed.*)

In both cases love was bursting through. The eternal was being realized in the present — and in both these instances it was human love!

And what of God's love? This passage of scripture says something quite remarkable: that God not only responds to prayer — he initiates prayer. He not only bends down to give help in the most trying of situations; he acts before we do. Through the Spirit he 'pleads' our cause.

How marvellous. How wonderful. God sees our need and comes to our help before we even ask. Is this what is meant by 'prevenient grace'?

> *Our advocate there*
> *By his blood and his prayer*
> *The gift has obtained,*
> *For us he has prayed, and the Comforter gained.*
> (Charles Wesley)

CREATIVE SUFFERING

Read Hebrews 12:7–11

Key verse: **When we are punished, it seems to us at the time something to make us sad, not glad. Later, however, those who have been disciplined by such punishment reap the peaceful reward of a righteous life.** (11)

As every physiotherapist knows, those who are recovering from a physical injury must be prepared to face the discipline of pain so that the injured limbs may perform their proper function again. As a hospital chaplain I have heard many elderly people complain about the discipline to which they are being submitted. 'Why don't they leave me alone?', they have said to me. 'I can't bear the pain.' But the good physiotherapist knows that they must not be left alone — to do so would be to condemn them to a living death. Pain now can give extended life with mobility tomorrow.

Similarly the psychotherapist knows that inner pain and hurt must often be experienced in all their depth and agony. Just to mask the pain and hurt with a psychotropic drug may, in the end, make matters much worse. Short-term aids, whilst sometimes necessary, cannot be long-term solutions. Psychic pain often has to be endured before it can be relieved. Like a good antiseptic, it has a job to do.

A good father cares for his children but he does not make excuses for all their misdemeanours and allow them to 'get away with it'. To do so would be to assist the establishment of patterns of behaviour which, in the long run, could prove disastrous. So with love and patience he applies 'discipline'. Happy is the son who can recall his father's restraining hand and realize that it was truly for 'his own good', although he resented it at the time.

How reassuring to know, in the darker periods of our lives, that God is treating us as his true sons and daughters (verses 7–8).

> *He'll never quench the smoking flax,*
> *But raise it to a flame:*
> *The bruised reed he never breaks,*
> *Nor scorns the meanest name.*
> (Isaac Watts)

CHOOSE LIGHT

Read John 3:14–21

Key verse: But whoever does what is true comes to the light, in order that the light may show that he did his works in obedience to God. (21)

One of the key concepts in John's Gospel is that of light. Jesus is the light of the world and many of the Johannine stories are to be seen as 'acted parables' demonstrating this truth.

Light, however, does two different things: it illuminates the way but it also shows up the dirt! The evil is revealed by the Jesus light for what it is — disobedience: failure to acknowledge God's supremacy or the Lordship of Jesus.

It is significant that the light spoken of in these verses streams from the cross. It was the suffering and uplifted Jesus who shed light and gave life.

A fascinating commentary on these verses comes from a twelve-year-old boy, Bob, who was born blind. Bright and intelligent, he reflected for a long time on his blindness and was especially frustrated when he lost his sense of direction. He was feeling particularly low one day when he thought of Roy Campenella, a baseball player, who was totally paralysed through a ball game accident. 'Campy', as he was known, could not even turn his own head. Bob said: 'I decided that the worst thing that could happen to a person isn't being blind or being paralysed. The worst thing is to lose all sense of direction in your life. I have often wondered what it must be like to see. I have never seen light. But if I have darkness around me all the time, I must learn to know that darkness . . . I think I do know it very well. Sometimes as a friend; sometimes as an enemy' (quoted by Elizabeth O'Connor in *Our Many Selves*, Harper & Row USA).

The light Bob discovered in his darkness was surely Calvary light. It was by accepting darkness that he was able to see beneath and beyond it.

> *O Lord, I cannot see!*
> *Vouchsafe me light:*
> *The mist bewilders me,*
> *Impedes my sight:*
> *Hold thou my hand, and lead me by thy side:*
> *I dare not go alone: be thou my guide.*
>
> (Jane Euphemia Saxby)

A STUDY IN CONTRASTS

Read Luke 18:9–14

Key verse: 'But the tax collector stood at a distance and would not even raise his face to heaven, but beat his breast and said, "God have pity on me, a sinner!"' (13)

The Pharisee illustrates *the unacceptable face of goodness*. No doubt he was a very good man. He did all the things he claimed. He was that kind of person. But in so doing he cut himself off from God because his satisfaction and his fulfilment lay in his achievements — in what he had become through what he did and did not do.

On the other hand the tax collector illustrates *the acceptable face of honesty*. He had nothing to hold up to God in order to secure his favour. He felt that he was an abject failure. Now when he realized the holiness of God, he knew that his cause was hopeless. There was only one thing left for him to do — to throw himself upon the mercy of God and ask for help and forgiveness.

Success; to be thought well of by a lot of other people; this is very nice. So nice that to strive for it unceasingly can become the subtle temptation that leads to hyper-activity and the inevitable breakdown in nervous and physical health which will follow.

Failure, however, which we all shun like a plague, can be the means of bringing us nearer to God and revealing life's true values. One day all our achievements are going to count for nothing. In the day of our testing when we stand before the King of Kings everything will depend upon what we have become as persons.

The tax collector was a failure — but the honest acknowledgement of his true condition pointed the way to a new and improved relationship with God. It always does.

> *Show me as my soul can bear,*
> *The depths of inbred sin;*
> *All the unbelief declare,*
> *The pride that lurks within;*
> *Take me whom thyself hast bought,*
> *Bring into captivity,*
> *Every high, aspiring thought*
> *That would not stoop to thee.*
>
> (Charles Wesley)

FROM DARKNESS TO LIGHT

Read Luke 7:36–50

Key verse: **'I tell you then, the great love she has shown proves that her many sins have been forgiven. Whoever has been forgiven little, however, shows only a little love.'** (47)

Those who refuse to acknowledge the darker side of their human nature and who deflect the challenge of evil forces, may live more peaceably, but they will be lesser people for having refused to confront these subtle enemies of Christian progress.

The woman in the story had an evil reputation. Everyone knew the kind of woman she was — and because of it she was openly despised. Yet here she was in company with Jesus; showering him with her expensive love-gift and washing his feet to the accompaniment of tears and kisses.

Such behaviour could not go unnoticed. The Pharisee who had invited Jesus to dinner began to think the worse of him. Did he not know that such women were to be despised? What was the Teacher thinking of to allow her to be so familiar with him?

Jesus 'read' the Pharisee's mind and heart. He knew just what he was thinking. He now tells the Pharisee the real truth. Yes the woman was a sinner, but she was a forgiven sinner. Grace had been at work in her life. Her depth and quality of love were in direct proportion to the sense of release she felt in being forgiven.

In order to live our lives in the fullest sense, we must not avoid difficulties and dangers. We shall all find that good and evil are intermingled in our lives. As we face our own dark shadows and allow the shame to bite we shall become all the more grateful to God that we have been forgiven. The experiences of failure have much to teach us about God's grace. They help us to be truly thankful that there is sufficient grace to meet all our needs.

How strong, O Lord, are our desires,
How weak our knowledge of ourselves!
Release in us those healing truths
Unconscious pride resists or shelves.

(F. Pratt Green)

CHRISTIAN TEMPTATIONS

Read 1 Peter 4:12–19
Key verse: **But if you suffer because you are a Christian, don't be ashamed of it, but thank God that you bear Christ's name.** (16)

Are there some subtle forms of temptation which tend to attack Christian disciples, perhaps after many years of going on in the faith?

How about refusing to acknowledge the existence of doubt? A personal religion which will not allow the admission of any sense of uncertainty is based on shaky foundations. Terrible things have been done (and still are being done) in the name of religion — cruelty, oppression, even murder. (Our critics have many sticks to beat us with.) But it is spurious religion — and it often seems to be based on absolute certainties. Or is it? Unacknowledged doubts emerge in a variety of ways and one of them is guilt, which is then repressed by appearing to be even more strong in one's convictions. This can lead to doing totally unchristian things in the name of religion.

Closely linked with this is unwillingness to admit the possibility of any future change of mind and heart. A saintly and scholarly Christian missionary who had worked among Moslem people for many years once surprised his students by saying that, in his dialogue with the Moslem people, he always kept open the possibility that he might become one of them. Defending this position he insisted that if his aim was to persuade them to become followers of Jesus, in all honesty he must keep open the option that it might in fact work the other way.

Becoming a Christian creates problems as well as providing clues to life's meaning and significance. The exciting thing about it is that when your faith is allowed to move and grow, problems are solved and more are created. This is part of the cost of discipleship — but it is energizing and uplifting and full of excitement.

> *When our confidence is shaken*
> *In beliefs we thought secure;*
> *When the spirit in its sickness*
> *Seeks but cannot find a cure:*
> *God is active in the tensions*
> *Of a faith not yet mature.*
> (F. Pratt Green)

REALISTIC CONFIDENCE

Read Romans 8:31–39

Key verse: **No, in all these things we have complete victory through him who loved us!** (37)

This week's readings end on a note of confidence — but also one of realism. If we are to understand that, in the end, nothing can separate us from God's love, then the implied suggestion is that many things will try to do so.

E. F. Schumacher (author of *Small is Beautiful*) offers us a clue when he suggests, 'The art of living is always to make a good thing out of a bad thing!'

Dietrich Bonhoeffer showed how this can be done. He knew at first hand all those experiences of which Paul was writing. What is more he chose to live with them. He could have remained safe and secure throughout the war in the USA teaching theology. Instead he lived his theology through danger, imprisonment, physical and mental suffering — and death! Here is a small extract from his *Letters and Papers from Prison* (SCM Press):

'It is only by living completely in this world that one learns to have faith . . . By this-worldliness I mean living unreservedly in life's duties, problems, successes and failures, experiences and perplexities. In so doing we throw ourselves completely in the arms of God, taking seriously not our own sufferings, but those of God in the world — watching with Christ in Gethsemane. That, I think, is faith, that is metanoia (repentance); and that is how one becomes a man and a Christian.'

It is when these things are actually happening to us that it is good to be reminded of God's ultimate assurance. His promises are never empty. He can and will bring us through life's varied events: pain and pleasure; joy and sorrow; freedom and imprisonment; living and dying. And through them all he is leading us onwards and upwards!

> *Though fiercest foes*
> *My course oppose,*
> *A dauntless front I'll show them;*
> *My champion thou,*
> *Lord Christ art now,*
> *Who soon shall overthrow them!*
> (Joachim Magdeburg)

HEALING THROUGH SUFFERING
Suggestions for group work

1. In one of the Bible readings the boy Bob who is blind says: 'But if I have darkness around me all the time, I must learn to know that darkness . . . I think I do know it very well. Sometimes as a friend; sometimes as an enemy'. Share your responses to this story. Is it ever possible to love the darkness?

2. Do you think that Frances Young's answer would be enough for you under similar circumstances? Discuss the quote: 'The absence of God and the presence of God. The agony of the world and the joy of the Kingdom. The one does not do away with the other, but it does transform it'.

3. What do you make of Hebrews 2:9–10? Does the fact of Jesus being made perfect through suffering have any relevance for us?

4. Go through the summary points at the end of this chapter. Check each statement and ask if it is true to anyone's experience.

CHAPTER FOUR

HEALING WITHIN DEATH AND BEREAVEMENT

The title of this chapter may sound somewhat ambiguous — but it has been deliberately chosen. It is about discovering God's healing grace *within* the process of dying and being bereaved. It is being written by someone who is in reasonable health and who has not known the searing pain of losing someone very close to him. Yes, my parents have both died, but they were old and I had lived away from home for many years. I loved them but their deaths were anticipated and accepted. I did not have to pass through a period of deep grief and mourning.

I know of course that I shall die, and being in my sixties I am aware that the period of time between now and my death is to be much shorter than the period between now and my birth! During that time I may lose someone I love dearly and so I do think about my own personal response to dying and bereavement. Indeed I think about it very often.

Through my work I have come to be with many people during the time when they became aware that they were dying — and I have sat and watched with them in the waiting room for death. I have held on tightly to people in the early paroxysms of grief, following upon a sudden death from accident or heart attack. I have often felt challenged by other people's courage, and I have wondered how I would respond in similar situations. I have not been at all sure.

As a minister of religion and an official representative of a church I am expected to have clear views on the 'proper' attitude towards death and to face it (my own and that of other people) fortified by my faith. I do have certain basic convictions by which I live, but I also have a number of unanswered questions. Some of the questions which I asked when I was younger have now been resolved in the light of experience. Others remain, but I believe that there are answers to them and that eventually they will be revealed. My reason for believing this can be best expressed in declaring what is my basic conviction: that God is love and that the purposes of love can never be defeated. It is love which lies behind creation. It is the knowledge that I am loved by God that has given meaning and significance to my life. I came to realize this through an awareness of the presence and power of Jesus. I seek to make daily contact with God and I am aware of the difference this makes to my inner sense of well-being.

This is what I have to offer as a Christian pastor but also as a human being. It does not give direct and specific answers to some of the questions people ask, like the natural question about what actually happens to me when I die. But I have found that to be honest with people and to share something of my real self with them is much more helpful than to give glib solutions to profound dilemmas when the so-called 'solutions' are not true to my own experience.

Facing our own dying

Victor Zorza is a well-known commentator on Soviet affairs who wrote for many years in the *Guardian*. His daughter became seriously ill and moved swiftly into a terminal state. She knew that she was dying and spent a number of weeks being cared for in a hospice. During that time she became convinced that she had to help her parents, and that she could best do so by encouraging them to face the reality of their own mortality.

After their daughter had died, Victor Zorza and his wife, who is also a writer, felt that they had to try to share what they had discovered about life and death through being so close to their daughter, and this they did in a series of newspaper articles and in a book. All their fees and royalties went to the hospice movement. In their writings they disclosed how richer they now felt life to be since they had walked in company with death. One thing, among many others, that their daughter had helped them to see was that the quality of life lived is of greater importance than its duration.

An Indian mystic, Anthony de Mello, suggests certain spiritual exercises in which we deliberately say goodbye to our own bodies by looking at every part and appreciating all that they have done for us. Hands, arms, legs, feet, eyes, ears — all have enabled us to enjoy varied aspects of our lives. He even suggests another exercise in which we deliberately see ourselves at the centre of our own funerals! Morbid? Perhaps it is not everybody's idea of a fruitful spiritual exercise — but it may help us to look deliberately at an event which is sure to come — and to see it not in negative but in positive terms. That is, to see death not as a point in life where everything is lost, but as a stage in being which opens out on to another stage, full of hope and new possibilities.

Healing and ageing

Because I write and speak about the churches' healing ministry and am also a working pastor, I sometimes find myself faced with a difficult pastoral encounter. An elderly person wants to talk to me about healing and how she can find help. As we talk I become aware that what she really wants is to be freed from the limitations of ageing and to go on living just as she always has done. I gently try to explain that the ultimate healing is that of dying and that God has created us in precisely this way. I can only seek to minister 'healing' if it is expressed in such ways as to ask God for his gift of greater 'wholeness' to be given to us in God's own way. I sense disappointment and am made to feel that this was not exactly what she expected!

Healing and wholeness are about finding completion and true fulfilment. We are born so that we might live, love, give birth, care for those given to us, eventually bid them 'bon voyage' — and die. Those who do find healing during their lifetime are surely healed in order that they may serve and, in the end, die a good death.

Death in hospital

Many people die in hospital in these days, although increasingly there are those who are able to spend their last weeks in a hospice. Those who do not have first-hand experience think of a hospice as being a place that is morbidly associated with death. In fact, the attitudes which are displayed in a good hospice have a great deal to teach us about life and how it might be lived.

Slowly 'hospice' ways of helping people in the final stages of their earthly lives are spreading to general hospitals but we have a long way to go. As a working chaplain I see people who are nearing the end of their lives in a hospital ward most weeks. Some things I find encourage me, but I am often disturbed.

The debate about whether or not to tell people the truth about their condition and to be realistic about the expectation of life goes on and on. Of course people differ and there is no blue-print as to how to deal with this most delicate and emotive of situations. But I sometimes wonder whose welfare comes first? Often it is the doctor who finds the task so difficult that he or she avoids it. Even the closest of relatives choose to live out a charade when the hours left could prove to be amongst the most precious of their entire relationship — and through which both might discover inward resources they never knew they possessed. Like most chaplains I have been asked, more than once, by a dying husband not to tell his wife that he knows that he is dying, and, by the wife, not to tell her husband the truth about his condition!

Those who work in hospitals naturally like to see people get well but this cannot always happen. If death is seen as failure then this feeling will spread to those most intimately concerned. 'He (the doctor) doesn't come and see me so often now', said a dying woman to me, 'and when he comes he never looks me straight in the eyes.'

How different a story I once heard from a patient who was fortunate to have a consultant who was not ashamed to reveal his true feelings. 'He asked to see me alone', she said; 'he sat on the bed, held my hand and quietly told me what the position was. I cried — and so did he. He promised before he left that he would not strive to keep me alive artificially and that he would see me through to the end.' He did!

When death arrives

Those who try to care for people know that when someone has died then the attention must switch to those who have lost someone they dearly love. A great deal has been written in recent years about bereavement and the various stages of grief have been analysed and outlined. It is useful to be aware of these stages so that you are not taken aback by the expressions of anger, guilt, remorse, apathy, self-pity and depression. There is no common pattern of course and these varied emotions appear, disappear and reappear. But the healing that eventually comes within the experience of bereavement is greatly helped by the willingness of friends and relatives just to 'be there'; to be available and to share in the process of grieving by allowing themselves to be used in the way each 'stage' requires. Anger in particular has to be understood. It is sometimes difficult to accept that you are the victim just because you happen to be around.

In the case of those who have died prematurely the question 'Why?' is often the first question to be asked. As a pastor I have often had to say, 'I'm sorry; I just don't know'. If the anger persists and it is directed against me because as God's personal representative (!) I ought to know, then I must just accept it and go on caring. An outburst of anger often ends in tears and caring is then best expressed by holding the person tightly in your arms. Later they may want to apologize but that doesn't matter. The anger may reappear later and the whole process be re-enacted.

The funeral

'The most important office you will ever conduct', said a lecturer in pastoral theology to his students, 'is a funeral.' Indeed a funeral does have an important part to play in the discovery of healing within the experience of bereavement. A funeral has been described as a 'rite of passage'. It helps people to accept separation; to prepare for a period of transition which then leads on to re-incorporation into a community in a new way.

The nature of a funeral will partially depend upon the kind of relationship which has previously existed between the priest or minister conducting the funeral and the person who has died. If there has been an established relationship, including regular visiting, in the period of illness which has led to death, then the situation is somewhat different from being asked to

44

conduct a funeral for someone you have not even seen. Nevertheless the same needs will exist in the lives of those most affected.

A funeral should always be a 'personal' occasion. Without being 'synthetic' or insincere, efforts can be made to discover something about the person who has died by pre-funeral visits and contact with friends. The use of the Christian name of the deceased helps to establish a warm and human relationship with the mourners. Elaborate eulogies are not called for but some simple expression of gratitude for the qualities of the person should surely be expressed. For many years I have included in each funeral service I conduct a period of silence, and ask each person present to use that silence to give thanks to God for those particular qualities and virtues they have come to appreciate in the life of their loved one, friend or colleague.

Every funeral provides an opportunity for a clear and plain expression of the Christian hope. I have discovered that to choose a different passage of scripture which seems in some way particularly appropriate to the occasion, saves me from the repetition of worn-out clichés. Somehow God seems to give to me the 'word' from within the 'Word'. Of course one also uses some of the familiar passages of scripture which help to provide a framework of security (Psalm 23; John 14; Romans 8) but to choose a particular passage for a particular person always seems to me to make for more effective communication.

Beginning again

The death of a life-partner, or someone equally close to you, is a traumatic experience, but given the opportunity to grieve and with the right kind of loving support, many bereaved people then move into a new stage of living. In some cases it is quite startling to see a person revealing qualities of leadership and initiative that even a happy marriage has somehow stifled. This does not necessarily reflect adversely upon the quality of the relationship which has now ended in death. The marriage may have been one in which the latent qualities now being revealed were not needed. Now they can blossom and flower within the new situation. Good bereavement counselling provides the opportunity to point out these possibilities and also to help individuals to cope with the guilt they sometimes feel when they discover that life is not over, but is becoming creative and meaningful again.

A woman known to me was affected deeply by the loss of her talented husband of whose life and influence she had been particularly proud. Then an opportunity came to her to exercise leadership in a local situation where there was a need. At first she declined, thinking that her late husband might not have approved. Eventually she accepted and this has led to her being offered a position carrying national responsibilities. One day she said to me,

'I hope my husband understands but my life now is as interesting and exciting as it was with him — it's just different!'

Resurrection

A friend of mine said to me recently, 'Lots of books have been written in recent years about dying and about bereavement but few of them seem to say anything about resurrection'.

He was right. It is important to recognize the difference between resurrection and revivification. Many people confuse the two. When we say in the Creed, 'I believe in the resurrection of the body', we are not referring to the body we know and live through in this life. 'If there is a natural body there is also a spiritual body' (1 Corinthians 15:44). The nature of that 'body' is one of my unanswered questions, but I look forward 'with hope' to a totally new form of being.

Clues to resurrection come in this life. We have already described an exciting new form of life opening up for someone following her recovery from the death of her husband. This could be described as a foretaste of resurrection. A marriage may be on the verge of break-up and through helpful counselling leading to deeper understanding and greater honesty, it can be 'resurrected'. We can die to some aspect of sin and failure in our lives and rise to new heights of Christian commitment which enables us to feel that we have been 'born again' into a new kind of existence.

Jesus is the resurrection and the life (John 11:25). He defeated the powers of darkness and is alive for evermore. He invites us to share in his resurrection and this happens as we entrust ourselves to him.

There is a basic simplicity about the Christian hope. There can be quiet confidence in its reality whilst, at the same time, there is agnosticism about its precise details. Here and now we do not possess the equipment to discern its true nature — but one day we shall (1 Corinthians 13:9–12). And of one thing we can be sure — our ultimate healing is bound up with our current and future participation in Jesus' resurrection life. And the more we are bound up with this *now* — the better we shall be prepared for the life to come. Remember: 'This is life eternal: to know thee, the only true God, and Jesus Christ whom thou hast sent' (John 17:3).

THE STATURE OF WAITING

Read Psalm 16

Key verse: **You will show me the path that leads to life; your presence fills me with joy and brings me pleasure for ever.** (11)

One of the experiences which comes to most of us in the later years of life is the change from independence to dependence. For years we have managed our own affairs and looked after ourselves. Now, slowly but surely, we have to rely on others. Eventually that relying upon others may become almost total.

There are ways of preparing for this time of waiting which comes to most of us sooner or later.

We can develop the grace of acceptance while we are totally fit and well. God's gifts of 'good things' (verse 2) often come to us through other people. I have known people who are always doing things for others but who will never allow anyone to do anything for them. How foolish! It may be more blessed to give than to receive — but it is blessed to receive.

We can deepen friendships and keep them alive by our positive attitudes towards our friends (verse 3). This is not to be thought of as an insurance policy but as a vital aspect of Christian discipleship. We are 'all bound up in the bundle of life' and we need each other.

W. H. Vanstone wrote a book called *The Stature of Waiting.* In it he shows how Jesus, having been the initiator of actions (see the early chapters of Mark's Gospel) then becomes the recipient of other people's activity. (Especially from the time of the events in the Garden of Gethsemane.) But in a very real way Jesus was still in charge of events even though what was happening to him was being decided by others. What was being done to him was all in the purpose of God and Jesus revealed his true stature and dignity by waiting on the world's activity and eventually showing how even the wrath of men can be turned to praise.

There are two different understandings of the word 'waiting' — the first in the sense of 'waiting' for something to happen, and the second in the sense of 'waiting' in prayer upon God. How does the one affect the other?

THIS IS THE REAL ME

Read Psalm 32

Key verse: **Then I confessed my sins to you; I did not conceal my wrongdoings, I decided to confess them to you, and you forgave all my sins.** (5)

The eminent psychological 'guru', C. G. Jung, once commented on the few Roman Catholics who had consulted him from among the many thousands of patients he had seen. Could this be because they are disciplined in the use of the 'confessional'? However the trappings of the confessional, with the anonymity of the 'box' and the mechanical nature of the directed 'penance', are unacceptable to many today — including some Roman Catholics.

Some Roman Catholic priests are encouraging their people to meet them 'face to face', in a counselling kind of relationship which then leads to their working out together a positive way of moving forward in the Christian life.

One of the experiences felt by some people facing death is a sense of guilt because of things not done and for which there is now little time left. Equally some people feel guilty following upon bereavement because they wish they had done more to improve the relationship between themselves and the person who has died.

A regular pattern of confession and forgiveness established in our day-to-day Christian lives can do much to avoid such guilt feelings. Happily we have a pattern established for us in the liturgy of the Eucharist. Always in this service there is opportunity for confession and the declaration of forgiveness. The challenge is to make the confession specific and real rather than formal and general. We need to feel our way into our own sin and failure and tell God about it. If we do this honestly then his forgiveness is assured.

Read the whole Psalm through again very slowly and pick out those sentences which seem to apply to your condition and to meet your need.

SPRING IN AUTUMN

Read Psalm 84

Key verses: **Happy are they in whose hearts are the roads to Zion. As they go through the bitter valley they make it the place of springs. The Autumn rains cover it with blessings. They walk with ever growing strength; they will see the God of gods in Zion.**

(5–7 Gelineau Version)

'He/she lived to a ripe old age.' Whenever you hear this said about anyone who has died what do you think is meant by the word 'ripe'? Does it simply refer to the length of life or does it have something to say about the quality of life lived by the person who has died? I think of the latter and certainly D. H. Lawrence does:

> It ought to be lovely to be old,
> to be full of the peace that comes of experience
> and wrinkled, ripe fulfilment.   (*Complete Poems*)

'Bitter valleys' come to most of us in a variety of ways. The psalmist tells us that it is possible to transform them so that they become 'the place of springs'. How?

Perhaps the clue lies in the phrase 'in whose hearts are the roads to Zion'. During the depression in Ireland they began to build roads to give the people something to do. They built roads out to towns and villages they believed would be built one day. But that day never came! They became 'ghost roads' which led to nowhere.

'Roads to Zion' are roads to God. They can be built by perseverance and by self-discipline. The cultivation of prayer-patterns which are adhered to even in times of spiritual dryness and doubt is one way of building such roads. In the day of testing and 'at the last day', such roads will lead us into the direct presence of the Father.

Which of your 'bitter valleys' need to be turned into a 'place of springs'?

Read Isaiah 35 and you will see the importance of 'building roads to Zion' in your own heart and life.

NO HIDING PLACE

Read Psalm 139

Key verse: **Lord, you have examined me and know me. You know everything I do.** (1 & part of 2)

'You know I lived with him for 45 years but I never felt that I really knew him.' This was what a woman aged over seventy said to me many years ago speaking of her husband who had just died.

Yes, such a relationship is possible and it is sometimes because of a deep-seated fear that someone close to you knows just how you are really feeling. Sometimes that fear exists on both sides and so there is collusion between the people concerned to keep each other at arms length. By this means they appear to live reasonably happy lives.

But the relationship could be much better and might indeed be improved by a 'showdown' in which barriers come down and masks come off. It would be painful but the consequences could be a new and revitalized relationship.

One thing is certain — God will not collude with us to enable us to live in an inadequate relationship with him. The Psalm makes this crystal clear.

The knowledge that God knows all can affect us in two different ways. *It can make us anxious.* There are things in our lives and particularly in our thoughts that we would like to hide from God. But this cannot be. If God is God then he is all-knowing.

But it can also reassure us. It can make us think about the real nature of God and when we do, with the help of the Psalm, it tells us that God not only *knows* but also *understands* us. Therefore we can be honest, open and relaxed with God and this will enable the relationship between us to be based, not on fear, but on trust.

To think about:
Our attitude towards God is bound up with our attitudes towards other people. In what ways might our personal relationships be improved by a new look at our relationship with God?

DEATH MEANS LIFE

Read 2 Corinthians 4:7–15

Key verse: **This means that death is at work in us, but life is at work in you.** (12)

Death and life are closely connected. This is an obvious statement but there is gold to be mined when you dig underneath and round about it. Paul was letting the Christians at Corinth know that he and his friends (the pioneers) lived in a dangerous world in which they daily 'dallied with death'. The forces of opposition were strong and powerful. They constantly harried those who witnessed for Christ. But the outcome of this was that a pattern had been established which was life-producing. Their inner spiritual energies were recharged as they identified in this life with the death of Jesus.

The benefits of their courageous stand were then made available to the Corinthian Christians. As Paul and his friends bore their trials so this added to the power of their witness and meant that 'life' was being generated in the Corinthian Church.

In Poland today the Catholic Church faces similar opposition. Sometimes it is subtle but often it is blatantly open and many priests and laity also 'dally with death' and some do die. Yet the flame of faith burns as brightly in Poland as ever it did. Brighter in fact than when the Church was politically favoured and influential in government circles.

One of their number, Father Calciu, says, 'I speak to you about death — it is your only hope of resurrection. Christ is risen and from this moment on your life has meaning. It will not finish up between the four sides of a coffin'.

Dag Hammarskjold once remarked: 'In the last analysis it is our conception of death which decides our answers to the questions life puts to us'.

In what ways am I dying to live?

V FOR VICTORY

Read Acts 17: 32–34
Key phrases: — **Some of them made fun of him.**
                — **Others said, 'We want to hear you again'.**
                — **Some joined him and believed.**

Paul was in Athens, where they loved to hear philosophic argument and debate. When he began to speak on Mars Hill he remembered this and began by adapting his style to theirs. But in the end he could not just offer philosophic generalities spiced with literary allusions. He raised the silver trumpet to his lips and declared:

— God has broken into history.

— God has raised Jesus from the dead.

— The whole human situation is changed.

— Righteousness is vindicated — darkness is defeated.

This was when the audience divided into three groups:

— some mocked;

— others wanted more time to think;

— some believed and joined his band of disciples.

Something similar happened to me over 35 years ago when I was preaching and speaking regularly in the open air. My style was to argue, debate, answer questions, and the best attended meetings were always those in which there was much audience participation! One night a young girl, with little speaking experience, mounted the platform while I was having a rest. She didn't argue. She didn't invite questions. She simply told the crowd that she believed in the resurrection because Jesus was alive and active in her heart and had transformed her life. The atmosphere was electric.

In the end experience counts. Yes, it must be based on reasonable intellectual foundations, but preaching is only effective when it includes testimony.

'What we have seen and heard
With confidence we tell.'

His resurrection and our experience of 'risen life' are intimately connected. What makes sense to you about resurrection — his and yours?

ALIVE FOR EVER

Read John 17:1–5

Key verse: **'This is eternal life: for men to know you, the only true God and to know Jesus Christ whom you sent.'** (3)

'Pie in the sky when you die.' This was how atheist critics used to caricature the Christian faith years ago. They were right to criticize the other-worldliness of a type of Christianity that turned people's eyes away from the squalor and poverty of their lot by assuring them that there would be rich treasure for them in heaven.

Nowadays most people in the 'Western' world have at least some 'pie' here on earth. However there is considerable fear of death and dying. What is it people fear? The physical fact of dying and the pain which might accompany it? To some extent this is true but the real raw nerve of human anxiety about death goes much deeper. It is about the ending of human relationships. All through our lives we are concerned to discover love — to receive it and to give it. But seldom do we find ourselves truly loved for what we are. Seldom are we able to give love just for its own sake.

Our loving then is often mixed up – a combination of selfishness and altruism. If however we can't find it at all, then we are likely to turn to a substitute — money, alcohol, popularity, drugs. But these are of little use because in fact they can be death-dealing. Either having them or not having them can lead to the same end. They are certainly not the answer to our inner loneliness.

What then is? The gospel is 'good news' because it does not talk about an eternal life that will be but that is. Eternal life is not about time as we know it. It is not about days and hours. It is about our real needs — being accepted and loved just as we are. Not first by other human beings but by the God who has revealed himself in Jesus. This is the only kind of life that really matters. In our relationship with God through Jesus we have a foretaste — 'the best is yet to be'.

Re-live a situation in which you did feel accepted, wanted, loved — for your own sake. Try and recall the way you felt when that happened. Then give thanks because what God provides is 'more than you can ask or think'.

HEALING WITHIN DEATH AND BEREAVEMENT
Suggestions for group work

1. Are we reluctant to talk about death? Has the way modern society deals with it caused us to lose something valuable? (Dying in hospital; funeral parlours, etc.) This may seem to be a loaded question calling for an obvious answer but it isn't meant to be. Talk around it.

2 'Death is a slice of life to be lived' (Michael Wilson). This is taken very seriously in a hospice. Share what you know about the hospice philosophy. (Questions answered honestly; pain minimized without loss of consciousness as long as is possible; cheerfulness combined with the acceptance of reality; opportunity for relationships to be 'completed'; an atmosphere which communicates 'life'.) How can what happens in a hospice help us now?

3. Should we be better prepared in our local churches for helping bereaved people? Can we cope with some of the anger which is often expressed, especially following upon a sudden death? How could we be better prepared? Make practical suggestions and, if you think it right, bring them to your Church Council, Elders Meeting or P.C.C.

4. Share your understanding of resurrection life. Be quite honest and, in particular, say what you find difficult about some traditional explanations. Say what you think is meant by the phrases in the Apostles' Creed, 'I believe in . . . the resurrection of the body and the life everlasting'.

CHAPTER FIVE

THE EUCHARIST AND HEALING

The late Lloyd C. Douglas, who wrote classics like *The Robe* and *The Magnificent Obsession,* once asked an old music teacher, 'Well, what is the good news for today?' The old man went over to a tuning fork suspended by a cord, struck it with a mallet and said, 'That my friend is "A". It was "A" all day yesterday; it will be "A" all day tomorrow and for a thousand years. The soprano warbles off-key, the tenor flats on his high note and the piano is out of tune, but that my friend is "A" and that is the good news for today' (*The Shape of Sunday* — a biography of Lloyd Douglas).

The Lord's Supper, the Holy Communion, the Eucharist, is like that note 'A'. It endures when all else fails. It remains in fashion when other modes of worship have had their day. It is the focal point of devotion, accepted as such by the overwhelming majority of Christian believers throughout the world — and it is a healing sacrament. Indeed the very pattern of wholeness we have been seeking after in the whole of this book so far is exemplified in the Eucharist.

We have already seen the importance of facing reality and we have considered the vital issues of suffering and death. We have also stressed the importance of 'balance' in the approach to the issues of health and healing. This 'balance' is to be found in paying careful attention to the total needs of people and offering help which takes into account their physical, mental, emotional and spiritual needs. Now we examine the structure of the Eucharist and make practical suggestions for its considered use in the ministry of healing.

The Eucharist celebrates the sacramental nature of the material

In some churches the Eucharist is celebrated with home-baked bread and home-made wine. Different families are invited to provide these material offerings and to bring them forward to be used in the service. I have shared in services when this has happened, and have felt that it adds to the rich symbolism of the occasion.

A wholesome loaf; a bottle of red wine — these are good illustrations of what can be achieved when we co-operate with God in his plan for his own world. We could not bake a loaf or produce a bottle of wine without God's help. He provided the original act of creation by which the basic materials came into being. When the rain and the sunshine have also played their part, human energy and skill make their distinctive contribution and, finally, bread and wine are offered at the Lord's Table — to be received back, when consecrated, as food to meet our deepest needs.

For a time now I have been associated with the Health Promotion Group appointed by our local Health Authority. Our role has been to encourage positive health practices. The menus offered within the hospitals have changed somewhat and patients are offered a more healthy variety of foods; a 'no-smoking' policy has been adopted and the practice of smoking discouraged on health service premises; general practitioners are being gently pressed into offering a variety of 'screening' processes to their patients. As yet we have not paid serious attention to the prevention and control of stress, but this will no doubt come. Mostly we have been dealing with health issues affected by the material properties of food, tobacco, and the like. We also want to stimulate growing interest in our personal responsibility for health through diet, exercise, relaxation, etc.

Sometimes as I have been celebrating Holy Communion I have deliberately had the work of the Health Promotion Group in mind and have offered it to God. As I have done so I have become aware of the sacramental nature of the materials we have been handling (through our thoughts and exchange of ideas and suggestions) in the Health Promotion Group.

The Eucharist is celebrated with material elements consecrated for holy service. By our participating we are giving thanks for the sacramental nature of all God's gifts — material and spiritual — and we are at the point where they are most gloriously combined.

The Eucharist puts us in our proper place

A vital element in every celebration of Holy Communion is the Act of Confession. Here we are invited to refer specifically to our sin against God and against our fellow men. This sin begins in thought and is then expressed in words and deeds.

The inward thoughts and feelings which can destroy our peace of mind and so affect our health in a variety of ways, are guilt, bitterness and resentment. Our guilt is sometimes artificial and may be due to our having contravened the boundaries laid down by our peers or our parents. Rationally we may be sure that our actions are justified, but inwardly and emotionally this may not be so. Skilled help with a counsellor or psychotherapist can often help us to escape from the effects of our irrational guilt. But not all guilt can be dealt with in this way. We are sinners (Romans 3:23). We do fail. It is right that we should feel guilty. There would be something wrong if we didn't.

Bitterness and resentment have corrosive effects upon the human personality. They smoulder away deep inside and wreak their havoc in our minds and bodies — and affect our capacity for spiritual experience. They can also make us most unattractive to other people. It is hard to cope with the person who has a continuous 'chip on the shoulder', even if sometimes there is justification for it.

The Eucharist provides a pattern for our release. We confess our sin and failure; we expose our bitterness and resentment; we repent. In response God forgives and the gracious promise of his forgiveness is contained within the eucharistic liturgy. Often the act of confession is more real if there has been some kind of counselling experience or simply talking things over with a trusted friend. For others there may be the opportunity of sacramental confession to a priest. Then the Eucharist provides the focal point both for confession and forgiveness.

Deep feelings of bitterness and resentment may call for some form of previous positive action. That action may be simply to accept that the feelings of injustice are right and proper. We have been treated badly by a colleague, employer or friend. Sometimes just to try and forget this is not possible. Some form of positive action is called for even if, in the end, there has to be acceptance.

That action might be to attempt to explore the issues with the person (or persons) concerned, perhaps with the help of a third party. It might even mean some form of organized effort to secure justice. There is no merit in being a doormat and allowing people to walk over you — they harm themselves as well as harm you by so doing. But finally, when all the avenues have been explored, there often comes the moment when the whole matter must be handed over to God. To continue to resent bitterly what cannot be changed does no good. If we bring it to God in the Eucharist the situation may not be materially changed but it can be specifically transformed!

In public life and in politics it is unfashionable to admit to failure or to ever being wrong. This can result in the most distressing and evil events like those still continuing in Northern Ireland. A bit of healthy repentance on all sides — and particularly from the extremes of the political divide — would do a power of good in that situation. A contemporary movement called 'Forgiveness in Politics' is trying to grasp this nettle. It badly needs grasping. If politicians would sometimes admit to being wrong it would enhance their standing in society and strengthen their credibility.

Repentance, sorrow for sin, the frank admission of failure, a deep desire for forgiveness; these necessities for healthy living are focussed in every celebration of the Eucharist. In that sense, among others, it is a health-giving exercise.

The Eucharist lifts us up to the heights

When the young Isaiah went into the Temple to pray to God to raise up a new king to succeed Uzziah, he was rewarded with a vision (Isaiah 6:1–8). He saw the holiness and majesty of God, became aware of his own need for cleansing and, when it came, heard God's direct call.

Every celebration of Holy Communion lifts up our eyes beyond the confines of ourselves until we see the majesty and wonder of God. Our liturgies for the Eucharist contain the Sanctus: 'Holy! Holy! Holy!' Isaiah's moment is ours. There is often too the Gloria. In this ancient hymn God is exalted, Jesus is praised for his role in taking away our sin, and the Holy Spirit acclaimed as binding all together in the one Godhead.

If it is necessary to become aware of our sin, it is also necessary to 'behold the glory of the Lord'. The person who is in touch with himself or herself, in touch with God and able to relate adequately to other people, must see beyond the limitations of this world and catch glimpses of the eternal. 'Where there is no vision the people perish' (Proverbs 29:18).

These uplifting experiences are to be enjoyed for their own sake but they make us infinitely more useful to God and to our fellow human beings. We rejoice also in those 'signs' of God's provision which we experience in music, art and literature. By them our whole beings are enriched and we are pointed in a Godward direction!

Similarly in the Eucharist we are reminded of our littleness and God's greatness. These two are constant but the recognition that 'communion' between the two is possible makes a profound difference to our total well-being in body, mind and spirit.

The Eucharist underlines our commitment to one another

This is dramatized when we pass the peace by making physical contact with our neighbours through a handshake or embrace and by speaking a word of loving greeting such as 'Peace be with you'. Some people do not like to pass the peace. They believe that religious faith is an entirely personal matter between themselves and God. Such a faith is not biblical. The earliest written record of the celebration of the Eucharist (the Lord's Supper) is in Paul's first Letter to the Corinthians (11:23–26). The passage immediately previous (17–22) deplores the divisions which existed within the Corinthian church, and the passage immediately following (27–34) warns against unworthy participation. Taken as a whole the entire passage (11:17–34) stresses the social nature of the Supper. It is clear that loving and caring relationships are an essential feature of the eucharistic feast. We shall see in greater detail in the final chapter how that they are also essential to the process of healing.

The Eucharist offers us life through brokenness

In the penultimate act before the bread and wine are received, the bread is broken. Thus we recall our Lord's sacrifice of himself for our sakes: 'He was wounded for our transgressions . . . by his stripes we are healed . . .' (Isaiah 53:5 and 1 Peter 2:24).

The liturgy speaks of 'his sacrifice and ours'. This concept of sacrifice is rooted in the Old Testament and the Jewish sacrificial system. A lamb was purchased, slaughtered and its blood sprinkled upon the altar. The worshipper thus identified himself with the sacrifice which had been made. It was a costly act and, having been reconciled to God, he ate the flesh of the lamb which had been offered.

But, as the Epistle to the Hebrews makes clear, what happened then was but a 'faint outline of the good things to come' (Hebrews 10:1). The supreme act of God himself was when 'Christ offered one sacrifice for sin, an offering that is good for ever' (Hebrews 10:12). This sacrifice was that of Christ's 'wholeness' and this was explicitly offered so that we might receive the gift of 'wholeness' direct from Jesus himself. As the modern hymn-writer, Fred Kaan, puts it:

> For the sacramental breaking,
> For the honour of partaking,
> For your life our lives remaking,
> Young and old, we praise your name.

So, when we come to the Lord's Table we claim his sacrifice and offer our own pain and frustration — and indeed our illness and disease — that what his sacrifice has achieved might become real and apparent in our own lives.

The Eucharist is the vehicle of our praise for blessings received

Praise and thanksgiving are essential elements in our quest for wholeness. In our intercessory prayer groups we often ask for specific blessings for individual people. When those blessings are given we do not always express our thanks as we might.

A retired minister I knew and loved was reaching the end of his days on earth. I used to visit him and pray with him. He was in considerable weakness and not a little pain. But I was always struck with two things about him — his continuing sense of humour and his capacity to be thankful. I went to minister to him but he always ministered to me. I came away chuckling at his jokes and marvelling at his deep sense of gratitude to God and to other people. The consultant who cared for him said that he had never met anyone else quite like him. They could and did talk together about life and death without any sense of strain.

To share the Eucharist with him was an uplifting experience. I always asked that we minister to each other. His extempore prayers of praise and thanksgiving will always live in my heart. He died as complete and 'whole' a person as I have ever known.

Some years ago a group of young people in my church wanted a name for themselves. They were a serious group meeting mainly for devotional purposes. One Sunday evening I preached on Colossians 2:6–7 with special emphasis on the final phrase, 'Be filled with *thanksgiving*'. I explained the word, '*eucharistia*' and used it a number of times. Afterwards they came to me and said, 'May we call our group "Eucharistia"?' I was hesitant at first, thinking of the association of the word with the celebrations of Holy Communion. But I could think of no good reason why permission should not be given. So for some considerable time the 'Eucharistia' group met after church on Sunday evenings. It was a happy group of young people who rejoiced in their Christian discipleship.

Those who grumble and grouse about life and who live with a constant 'chip on their shoulders' will never find true health and wholeness. Gratitude and thanksgiving are essential features in the full and radiant life. As we share in the regular eucharistic celebrations we have the opportunity to take stock and to give thanks. It is a healthy and life-giving activity.

The practical consequences

Those who minister healing have discovered, through experience, that the Eucharist plays a significant role in the healing process. 'Because Holy Communion is a continual remembrance of Christ's great healing life, death and resurrection, in which all participants receive the life-giving Spirit, it is a healing service' (R. A. Lambourne in *Community, Church and Healing*, DLT but out of print).

☐ The Eucharist provides a perfect setting for the laying on of hands and/or anointing. We have already seen that the structure of the service provides a framework for an expression of Christ's offer and our response. The laying on of hands with or without anointing seems to follow on quite naturally and is a further 'means of grace'. Those who desire this additional ministry can remain kneeling at the communion rail when they have received Holy Communion. They can then be ministered to in this way by a small group of people. This helps to emphasize the corporate nature of this act. If only one person acts there is always the danger of people thinking that the healing power lies in the hands of the person rather than with Christ, the Head of the Church and the Lord of the Feast.

☐ Dr Kenneth P. McCall has written a remarkable book called *Healing the Family Tree* (Sheldon Press). He makes special reference in the book to the long-term effects upon those who have had still-born children for whom there has been no 'rite of passage'. He says: 'I have over six hundred recorded cases of direct healing which has taken place after a Eucharist has been celebrated for babies who were either aborted, miscarried, still-born or discarded at birth and who have never been properly loved or committed to Jesus Christ in a burial service.'

In recent years I have become aware myself of the importance of a 'completing rite' to take place for a still-born child. Nowadays much more attention is given to the parents at this time and, in the hospital where I am currently a chaplain, we have laid down a procedure to make sure that every parent facing this kind of trauma knows precisely what is available to them. Pastoral sensitivity is called for as this is a time of extreme emotional distress, especially for the mother.

☐   The work of Dr McCall is closely related to what has become known as 'the healing of the memories'. Emotional disturbances in early childhood often leave wounds which may begin to fester much later in life. After careful medical diagnosis to eliminate possible physical reasons for the disturbance, counselling or psycho-therapy can help to bring those memories to the surface. But that does not mean necessarily that their disturbing power has been eliminated or even curtailed. Many involved in pastoral care find that to bring those memories and by-gone experiences directly into a Eucharist which has been specially arranged for the occasion often has powerful therapeutic effects. If those who have been helping in the care of the person mainly concerned can be encouraged to share in the service, this is an additional benefit and often helps them, as well as the person whose needs are placed at the centre of the Eucharist.

Charles Venn Pilcher sums it all up for us in his communion hymn:
> Here, Lord, we take the broken bread
> And drink the wine, believing
> That by your life our souls are fed,
> Your parting gifts receiving.
>
> As you have giv'n, so we would give
> Ourselves for others' healing;
> As you have lived, so we would live,
> The Father's love revealing.

PUT FLESH ON THE WORD

Read John 1:1–14

Key verse: **The word became a human being (became flesh) and lived among us. We saw his glory, full of grace and truth.** (14)

It is a simple story and it really did happen. Many years ago a saintly lady belonging to a church of which I was minister had access to an unending supply of biscuits. This was because her friend and companion who lived with her worked in a biscuit factory and was able to buy very cheaply the ones which were slightly damaged. Now this lady was also a church visitor, and whenever she visited a family she would take with her a small gift of a packet of biscuits. One of our couples, who had been regular attenders at worship, suddenly stopped coming. They had taken offence at something or other and showed their displeasure by staying away! I had been to see them but to no avail. So I played my trump card. I sent Miss M.

Soon they were back. Explanation? 'Nothing to do with you at all', they said. 'It was Miss M. She came to see us every week and each time she came she brought us some biscuits. She seemed to be telling us that we still mattered and that somebody cared for us. In the end it was the biscuits that did it!'

My mind flew to this verse from John 1: 'The word became flesh'. A woman's faithfulness and the odd packet of biscuits. The sacramental nature of a simple act. The material offering which conveyed a spiritual blessing.

These verses in today's reading contain some of the profoundest thinking in the entire New Testament. They come to us through the mind of the beloved disciple, John, after he had spent years reflecting on the wonder of the Incarnation. He had also become familiar with the practice of breaking bread and drinking wine as a constant reminder of that Last Supper and, along with his fellow believers, he had found in this act a rich means of grace.

Food for thought:

— Jesus was God's Word who became flesh — to show us the way to God.

— We are invited so to receive Jesus daily into our own hearts and lives and then, by our words and deeds — to put flesh on to the Word!

SORRY, LORD

Read Psalm 51

Key verse: **Sincerity and truth are what you require; fill my mind with your wisdom.** (6)

Everyone has some secrets. There are some aspects of our lives we have never shared with anyone. This is both natural and normal; we are all entitled to some inward privacy. But sometimes the nature of our closely guarded secrets does us harm. We worry about them. We are gripped with a sense of guilt. We wish that the events had never happened.

Our guilt may disturb our rest. Our anxiety may affect our digestion. Our bitterness may bring about strange aches and pains. Our 'living in tension' may affect our blood pressure.

Every day thousands and thousands of prescriptions are made out by doctors to help people to live with their symptoms. This is all these drugs can do. They can help us get through a difficult period. They are palliatives which bring some measure of relief. But they are not the real solution to the problem. They do not get to the root of what is going on deep inside us.

The circumstances which gave rise to this Psalm are familiar: uncontrolled desire; trickery to gain one's own ends; murder! But David had not reckoned with the courage of Nathan (see 2 Samuel 12:1–15). David felt the full impact of his own conscience. He was the king but even he was subject to a greater law and a more powerful Overlord!

But David's sorrow is real. His repentance rings true. He was helped to see that it is what goes on in the depths of a person's inward being which affects his whole personality. He could not shuffle his responsibility off on to anyone else. He was the man.

Food for thought:

 Let the Psalm speak for you and express some of your thoughts and feelings.
 — All sin is ultimately against God (4).
 — He alone can create a clean heart (10).
 — Praise associated with confession is acceptable (15).
 — Requests can come when confession and praise have taken place (18).

VISION ON!

Read Isaiah 40:12–31

**Key verse: To whom can the holy God be compared? Is there anyone
else like him?** (18)

After living in London for a quarter of a century I came to live on the edge of
the Lake District. From my study window I can see the tops of the
mountains. Whenever I can I get out on to the fells and, if there is time, climb
a mountain. Although I always go with my wife, I like to have time on our
walks to be alone. I want to feel the bigness of the mountains; feel their
strength and solidity, marvel at their rugged beauty. I want to get that vision
firmly implanted in my mind so that when I leave the mountains they will
never leave me.

When Paul was arrested by the Spirit of Jesus on the Damascus Road
(Acts 9:1–19), he went blind. It seems that he had to spend a period in
darkness so that the full significance of what had happened could dawn upon
him. Then when his eyes were opened his heart and mind were inspired and
prepared. From that point on he was ready to . . .

> Serve with a single heart and eye,
> And to thy glory live or die. (Charles Wesley)

Here is a pattern for a growing Christian life in which we move towards a
greater wholeness. First we 'see the Lord'. This may come about as we face a
particular challenge; it may come through an inspiring thought; it may
happen within the Eucharist itself.

Then follows a period of reflection upon what has happened. This may
take a little time; it is not always clear what God is saying to us in the high
moments of our lives. A retreat may be called for when we go away to some
quiet place where the full import of our vision can be analysed, and we can
ask God to make the way ahead clear and plain.

Finally there is the resolve — the decision to act and the initial steps in a
new adventure.

Food for thought:
— *Read the passage suggested through again.*
— *Ask God to use it to clarify your vision.*
— *Notice the promise right at the end of the passage.*

LOVE SMELLS NICE!

Read Philippians 4:10–20

Key verse: **. . . your gifts . . . are like a sweet-smelling offering to God, a sacrifice which is acceptable and pleasing to him.**　　　　　(18)

Here we have an opportunity to listen in on a conversation between Paul and the Philippian Christians. It is contained in this intimate, personal letter which illustrates the importance of caring for one another in down-to-earth, practical ways.

The passage sheds light on the character of Paul. He seems to want to insist that his needs are few. He doesn't want to live in any kind of luxury but nevertheless he values the luxury of the assurance of their love for him.

It wasn't only the gift that pleased Paul; it was the warmth of the thought which lay behind it. But that wasn't all. In addition it was an indication to him of the growing faith of his Philippian friends. He was delighted that they were 'going on' in the faith and making good progress.

Dr Martin Israel suggests that 'The measure of a truly spiritual healing is the steady transformation of the person's character so that he ceases to live for himself alone but gives himself even more unreservedly to others' (in *Healing as Sacrament*, DLT).

Food for thought:

— *When we share what we have we do ourselves a power of good; we enlarge our own lives and characters. We don't share just for this reason, but it is a welcome by-product.*

— *When others share something of themselves or their substance with us, let us be thankful and appreciative. Paul cemented the relationship between the Philippian Christians and himself through his genuine thankfulness.*

— *Recall when you last received or gave 'a sweet-smelling offering'.*

LONG LIFE BREAD

Read John 6:25–35

Key verse: **'Do not work for food that spoils; instead work for food that lasts for eternal life.'** (27)

Bread — in all its different forms — is the staff of life. One of the tragedies of the twentieth century is that we have developed human skills to levels of sophistication which take the breath away and cause us to marvel at the ingenuity of man, yet, at the same time, we allow millions to starve and die for lack of bread!

It is significant that the bread of which Jesus speaks in this passage is the 'bread of life'. Bread does generate life. It symbolizes the protein, carbohydrate, vitamins and minerals which are required for growth and renewal. Our bodies are changing throughout our lives and this process depends upon the nourishment provided by sufficient food. The experts tell us that, given the political will, we could provide adequately for everybody, but it is precisely that motivation which is missing!

Is there a connection between our being fed week by week at the Lord's Table and the aching human need which surrounds us in the wider world?

There must be, but perhaps it is that we should not allow ourselves to be overwhelmed by the magnitude of the task and by the feeling that we are not able to do very much about it. Jesus seems to have met human need as he could wherever and whenever he came into contact with it. He shared himself with people in such ways that they came alive in the fullest sense. In addition he challenged the leaders and rulers he met and this led to his death.

Food for thought:
— *Bread is meant for sharing.*
— *If we stockpile our bread it will go mouldy.*
— *Public opinion shapes political decisions and we are public opinion!*

A FRIEND OF JESUS

Read 2 Corinthians 5:16–20

Key verse: **When anyone is joined to Christ he is a new being; the old one is gone, the new one is come.** (17)

It is possible to be acquainted with Jesus yet not to relate to him as friend. It is possible to tell others about Jesus but without any sparkle or fire. Then something happens which makes you think as you have never thought before.

Around 1968 I became acquainted with the work of Alan Dale. He had written a free translation of parts of the New Testament which was published first in five separate volumes for schools, and later in one volume entitled *New World*. Since that time it has become one of the most used volumes on my shelves. Through reading it I began to enjoy the New Testament as never before. It came alive with a relevance and meaning which had hitherto eluded me.

One of the key phrases he uses is 'the friends of Jesus' and this phrase came to mean much to me. I was a friend of Jesus! What a wonderful privilege! What an awesome responsibility!

The result was that I began to feel better. I began to do my work with greater zest. I was much more integrated as a person.

This is one of the ways healing comes — through integration. Through feeling that you have made contact with a point at the heart of reality which holds everything together. This is surely what Paul is saying in our key verse. And if there is a key word in our key verse it is surely 'joined'. We are part of him and he is part of us.

Food for thought:

— *Each time we come to the Eucharist our awareness of that power at the centre is rekindled.*

— *The friends of Jesus are charged to introduce others to share his friendship.* (18)

— *He has provided the equipment for us to do this.* (20) *Are we making use of it?*

PROFIT AND LOSS

Read Acts 16:16–24

Key verse: **Paul became so upset he turned round and said to the spirit, 'In the name of Jesus Christ I order you to come out of her'. The spirit went out of her that very moment.** (18)

Exploitation of human frailty goes on today as it did then. We may be more humane in our treatment of the handicapped, but they are still an underprivileged section of society, as the relative sums expended upon meeting their needs through public funds indicate. The girl with an evil spirit was 'owned' by those who were making money out of her. It was only when their pockets were hit that they became angry and took action.

Paul called on Jesus for the girl's deliverance and it happened immediately. One moment she was shouting; the next moment she was quiet and subdued.

Exorcism is an area where we must tread carefully. Wonderful things do happen 'in the name of Jesus' but not always suddenly as in this story. Sometimes they happen slowly and quietly through caring people co-operating to help a person in deep emotional need.

A vital factor in the healing process is always love. When people in need feel that they are loved wonderful things happen to them and they express it in different ways. 'I feel all warm inside', said one. 'I feel unbuttoned', said another, 'as though I have stepped out of a tight corset which held me in its grip.'

As we have seen in the chapter preceding these Bible readings, to bring specific situations of need in relation to individual people, into the heart of a Communion Service, can be a means of real blessing. Often the improvement is slow. The people concerned feel a need to re-live what took place in 'their' Communion Service by attending the regular celebrations in their own church. But the love which they feel streaming from the heart of Jesus can melt away the icy coldness they feel at the centre and bring them warming release.

Food for thought:

— *Paul and Silas paid the price of their actions by being beaten and thrown in jail. Sometimes today to care is costly.*

— *Their 'loss' however brought 'profit' to the girl and also to them because through being in prison they were given a new opportunity to witness. (See Acts 16:25–32.)*

— *Martin Israel suggests that the two requirements for a healing ministry are an openness to God and a deep concern for other people.*

THE EUCHARIST AND HEALING
Suggestions for group work

1. Basic to this chapter is the idea that the Eucharist offers the pattern for a healthy way of life — penitence, vision, commitment to each other and to God, etc. Had you ever thought of this before? Does the pattern have anything to say about health care generally and the way it is provided?

2. Do we make any particular provision in our church(es) for people to share experience and deliberately to practise loving, caring relationships? (Does this turn you on or off?) Should we encourage groups for this purpose? What are the potential dangers? What are the possible benefits?

3. Does the idea of celebrating a Eucharist to meet a special need appeal to you? Should you consider whether your group should make any positive suggestions about it to the 'powers that be' in your church(es)? Have you any experience of the long-term effects of loss through miscarriage, still-birth, etc.? (Be careful because if any member of the group has had an actual personal experience such discussion could be traumatic.)

4. Are we reluctant to use the tools God has given us (of which the Eucharist is one) in the healing process? In what ways could our eucharistic worship become more relevant to people's actual needs?

CHAPTER SIX

HEALING
AND COMMUNITY

The quality of life enjoyed in any given community has a direct bearing on the health standards of those who live within it. As we have already seen briefly in our Introduction, social policies and their political implementation have had a profound effect upon health standards. Humane laws on shop, office and factory conditions have added to the improvements which followed from purer water supplies and public health measures governing the way food is processed, stored and offered for sale. This kind of social legislation, combined with educational enlightenment, has been responsible for distinct improvements in health and well-being. A number of commentators on social development agree with T. McKeowen writing in *The Role of Medicine* (Nuffield Trust) that such measures have actually done more to improve health than medical advances and improved medical technology.

A vivid illustration of the way in which a breakdown in community life affects health standards has been provided for us by the miner's strike in the United Kingdom in 1984/85. Lasting for a year it resulted in the division of communities because the miners were not all of one mind. In some areas working miners outnumbered striking miners; in other areas striking miners were very much in the majority. Then as time wore on areas which had seen solid support for the strike saw the emergence of groups of men determined to return to work. It was this which caused the greatest bitterness and the consequences will be felt for years to come.

The effects upon the health of individuals in the communities was significant. Physical violence with its psychological damage to those at both the giving and receiving ends did much harm. The surgeries of the general practitioners were crowded with people suffering from nervous tension, anxiety, sleeplessness, stomach and bowel complaints. The effects upon children were marked: behaviour problems in schools, bed-wetting, headaches, etc. Among the psychological symptoms was unhealthy withdrawal caused by threats and fear. Some families which were part of small minority groupings felt that they could not remain in communities in which they had lived all their lives and sought new jobs and new homes in what they hoped would be more friendly new areas.

New town 'blues' and high rise depression

New areas, however, present their own problems. Whenever communities have been created rapidly on new housing estates and in new towns, health problems have occurred. I recall the rash of high-rise flats built in East London in the sixties when vast numbers of people were being re-housed from sub-standard accommodation. The physical conditions in which the people were now living were, at first, a vast improvement on what they had previously known. However, totally insufficient attention had been paid to how families would *feel* in their new surroundings. The dangers of stairs and lift-shafts and the inadequate play areas for children, all added to the problems. When the group of churches with which I was associated set up a family support service we were inundated with clients. The upper floors of high rise flats had splendid views, but their isolation created an aching loneliness which made many of the occupants long for the friendly squalor of the slums.

Middle class pressures

It is not easy to quantify the amount of ill-health caused by the desire for status symbols and possessions, but it is considerable. R. A. Lambourne puts it in this way: 'A man's peptic ulcer demonstrates not only the deficiencies in the structure of the wall of his duodenum . . . He may be bearing about in his body the ulcer of his wife's ambition to keep up with the Joneses, which in turn reflects childhood experiences of poverty and grave social injustice'.

At every level the nature of community life affects health and well-being. When a mother takes her child to the doctor she describes the child's symptoms as she has become aware of them but, as often as not, the root of the problem lies in the relationships existing in the family of which they are both a part. Many nervous illnesses and their physical consequences are the result of family difficulties, neighbourhood problems, and of course, unemployment.

The nature of response

Different people react differently to the same kinds of pressure. Unemployment drives one man into the depths of despair. In another it triggers abilities he never knew he possessed. A man I know whose redundancy fired him to begin his own small business now refers to the experience as being 'the best thing that ever happened to me in my life'. It became for him a growth point but he was a person with considerable mental and spiritual resources. Recalling Michael Wilson's definition of health as being able 'to respond in a mature way to life as it is', we may say that the opposite is also true. Responding in an *immature* way to life as it is creates problems and causes illness.

The response then to community-oriented illnesses has to be on two levels: the first is to help the individual to cope better with his or her new situation; the second is to try to improve the social situation itself by striving to create healthier forms of community life.

In any attempt to help individuals (medical, pastoral, psychological or ideally a combination of all three), the positive side must not be overlooked. There is a natural urge to maintain equilibrium and each individual possesses vital healing resources within himself or herself. Those who are trained to help others to become more in control of their own situations, know the value of concentrating upon enhancing strengths as well as trying to deal with weaknesses. Nevertheless many are overwhelmed because their inner resources are inadequate to cope with the effects of their depressing social environment.

Community development strategies

Improving community situations can be attempted in a variety of ways. One well-tried method is the introduction of a trained community development worker into a defined area. He or she seeks to mobilize the community strengths which already exist and then seeks to be a catalyst for the development of new ventures which the people themselves undertake. The idea is for the community development worker to function in such ways that eventually he or she is no longer necessary.

In the under-developed parts of the world village health workers function on this kind of principle. With the help of some basic training in hygiene, water purification, maternity care and disease prevention, plus access to some simple basic drugs, the village health worker is able to release the resources which exist within the people themselves. Often they find it possible to work in co-operation with the native 'healers'. Some of the simple herbal remedies and mind therapies which have been practised for generations can still be of help to those who have not been influenced by Western expectations. Missionary Societies, which have often pioneered medical work in more primitive society, are discovering that money invested in such health workers pays much higher dividends than building Western-style, high technology hospitals. Of course such hospitals are needed for certain types of illness but a large cross-section of health needs can be met at village community level.

Community health pioneers

In Britain some pioneers are seeking to put the same principles into action (albeit in more sophisticated ways) in front-line medical care. Progressive doctors are forming self-help groups within their practices. Particular needs are met by people with similar problems (obesity, difficulty in stopping smoking, anxiety, etc.) being brought together in groups to help one another.

Working in co-operation with 'good neighbour' schemes they are making sure that the elderly and chronic sick are cared for as long as possible within the community itself. 'Health is everybody's business', they insist. The idea that only 'professionals' can deal with health problems really will not do. The professionally trained can share their skills with others in ways which are appropriate. When people are trusted and helped to help themselves they develop a confidence and maturity which is a sure sign of improving health. Healing can come about as the result of feeling that you are part of a co-operative enterprise. Health is not delivered in packages, nor is healing, but both health and healing can be enabled. (For information about what is being done in an actual situation write to the Templegarth Trust for Health Cultivation, 82 Tinkle Street, Grimoldby, Louth, Lincs. LN11 8TF.)

A hospital points the way

The same principles can apply in hospitals, even in departments where serious illness like cancer is being treated. In Glasgow for instance there is a hospital where cancer patients, their relatives, staff at all levels and former patients, get together to share their experiences, their fears, their anxieties — and their hopes! The Professor in charge, who has himself originated the programme, describes it as providing a 'never ending bucket of love' from which all may have to draw (including himself), and to which all may contribute.

In hospitals for nervous illness there has for many years been an approach based on the concept of the therapeutic community. This consists of a series of groups in which doctors, patients, nurses, chaplains and occupational therapists, etc. all meet together. Openness is encouraged and people are invited to care for one another. The idea that one section of the group possesses skills which are dispensed to the other is unacceptable. The aim is to facilitate each person's skill in the art of living. Sometimes the patients act as 'enablers' and sometimes it is the full-time professionals. Often patients are helped by one another. The concept is that all have needs and out of mutual vulnerability hope can be born and progress made.

A Christian response

Whenever positive steps are taken to promote human maturity and to enrich the quality of people's lives, there will be rising standards of health and men and women will find healing. This is Christian whether or not it is done in the name of Christ. However this whole book is about Christian initiatives and its aim is to provoke thought and action which will promote health and enable healing.

The Rev. William Gowland of the Luton Industrial Mission was one of the pioneers of industrial mission and he has repeated many times that 'you cannot redeem what you do not understand'. The same is true of our approach to health and healing, which in one sense is an industry. The aetiology (causation) of disease is a complex and difficult question. Medicine utilizes many scientific principles but it is a combination of art and science and not a pure science as such. The reason for this is that the doctor is working with people who are all different. A diagnosis of a disease affecting one person may be the same as the diagnosis for another. Yet the same treatments for both people will not necessarily achieve the same results. The reason is that both the onset of disease, and the way in which individuals respond to treatment, are both determined by the nature of the sick person — their 'balance'; their equilibrium, their integration, their ability to develop and use spiritual resources.

We must therefore tread carefully and be ready to utilize all the help and skill we can find to help men and women to find richer, fuller and more exciting life-styles which, in the end, will pay off in increased ability to discover the wholeness which is an integral factor in health and healing.

However, we can and do claim that there is a powerful Christian contribution which can be made both in understanding what true health is, and in providing resources to enable healing and growth to take place.

The body of Christ

Recent years have seen developments in liturgical and biblical understanding which place great emphasis upon the importance of the body of believers. This 'togetherness' is focussed in the Eucharist and, as we have seen in the previous chapter, this central service of faith has a vital healing role. When we are together we feel the strength of the community of faith, but when we are together 'in Christ' this adds a new dimension. We are not only loving and supporting one another — this is good in itself — we are drawing upon the body of Christ through the Eucharist and thus becoming more part of the 'body of Christ' which is the church.

This means that we have a greater grasp of the 'wholeness' of Jesus and thus we are made more 'whole' ourselves. On the occasions when I have celebrated a Eucharist for a sick person and then laid hands upon them along with a group of friends or family, I have been conscious of the 'real presence' in a unique and significant way. Renewal has come both through a new grip on life or an easy and meaningful death.

The sharing group

To raise up a joyful act of praise to the Lord and then to stream forward to the Table to receive the bread and wine is a joyous experience. Many however feel that this needs to be complemented by the existence of small groups, within which individuals can be themselves, and express their feelings as well as their thoughts and ideas. For a number of years I belonged to such a group. We laughed together, cried together, prayed together and, when those of our number passed through dark waters, literally and physically held on to one another. It was a group which crossed the boundaries of church loyalties and it included people of widely different personalities. Most of us would say that through the group we found healing in one way or another. I know I did.

The prayer group

This can be a sharing group as well but it may be a group of people who give themselves in a disciplined way to God on behalf of other people and particularly those in need. Such a group can be a powerful influence in the life of any church or community. Those who participate in them will tell you that they feel closely linked with those who are being prayed for and through them, more closely linked with God. The purpose of such a ministry of intercession is not to change God's mind nor to bring things to his notice, but to put those in need in that place where God can bless them. We stretch out one arm to God and the other, in our imagination, to the person concerned.

One point worth making about such a group is that it is not made up of the spiritually élite and it is usually fairly small. Those who feel God calls them to share in this ministry do it representatively on behalf of the whole church community. Having had such a group active in my churches over the last twelve years I know the blessing and help it has been to many — not least to me!

Into the world

You cannot just pray for people if you know they are lonely and needing a friend. You cannot just put their name on a prayer list if they are sick and need some practical help in cleaning the house or doing the washing! Prayer and service go together. The Lord's Table and the kitchen sink can both be places where Holy Communion is celebrated. Sometimes with bread and wine and sometimes (and I mean this reverently) with dirty dishes. After all this was one of the ways in which Brother Lawrence met with God.

The church *is* healing

This was a title of an early book written by Michael Wilson. It simply meant that if the church community is truly centred in Christ then through it healing will come. The criterion by which we discern a healing church community comes direct from our Lord himself: 'By this shall all men know that you are my disciples, that you love one another'. And through our love for one another healing spreads from the church community out to the wider community. The community of faith enables healing to take place in the community — by the community — and through the community. And it happens because, within that community, love is sought, nourished and shared.

FRIENDLY PERSISTENCE

Read Mark 2:1–12

Key verse: **Jesus saw how much faith they had, and said to the paralysed man, 'My son, your sins are forgiven'.** (5)

He had friends. The healing could not have taken place without them because the paralysed man could never have got near to Jesus. But having been motivated to take their friend to meet the healer they had to overcome another set-back. The crowds prevented them getting anywhere near. But they had come so far and they were not going to be beaten. They made a hole in the roof.

He had inward needs. His physical paralysis was associated with his state of mind and heart. Jesus broke through into that inner citadel as only Jesus could. He told him plainly that his sins were forgiven. Then the paralysis left him.

He accepted some responsibility for himself. When Jesus told him to get up — he did. He did not even raise a hand for help although presumably his friends were still near and available. He didn't even ask them to pick up the bed!

The people praised God. They were right to do so. We take so many things for granted — including healings from whatever source and by whatever means our healing comes. We take health for granted — until we become ill. Then we realize what a precious gift good health is. An attitude of thankfulness which gives rise to praise of God from time to time is a healthy activity in itself.

Re-live this parable within your own church and community situation.

— Am I — along with my Christian friends — so motivated that we take those in need right into the presence of God? How do we do it? Have we the persistence to overcome obstacles?

— Do I realize how much my inward state affects my physical body? In what areas of my life am I paralysed? How does this affect my activities in church and community?

— Do I/we spend enough time in honest thanksgiving? Toyohiko Kagawa used to suggest that we begin from one hundred and then say, 'I haven't got a car so I have 99 things left'. Just go on taking away until you come to the point where you realize how many blessings you have. Then give thanks.

RICHER LIVING

Read Romans 12:1–8

Key verse: **So then, my brothers, because of God's great mercy to us, I make this appeal to you: Offer yourselves as a living sacrifice to God, dedicated to his service and pleasing to him. This is the true worship that you should offer.** (1)

The implications of this superb chapter (Romans 12) will takes us not two days (as in these notes) but a lifetime to absorb. Here in the first half of the chapter is a vivid description of Christian community life which, if discovered and lived, is bound to affect the wider life of the community in which it is set.

☐ *Inward transformation* (2). This is where it all begins. As individuals are renewed, directions are changed, values re-assessed, people look inward to God and then outward to other people. Corporate life then becomes supportive and enriching rather than totally demanding, draining us of our inner resources. This new life fires communities and provides the energies for an ongoing, Spirit-inspired, life which makes a powerful witness in society.

☐ *Proper view of self* (3). When individuals are helped by the group to which they belong to formulate reasonable judgements upon themselves, the results can be creative. Communities do suffer from people who are over-bearing — but also from people who refuse to develop their potential by what they describe as proper modesty but which is really timidity, insecurity and fear.

☐ *Serving and Sharing* (7). This is how we grow and in this connection it is motivation that counts. If we serve and share because we are responding to a social norm our activities will be formal and lack grace. The one adequate motivation is gratitude.

Be daring! Ask God to use this passage to point you to new possibilities. They might include . . .

— A higher level of consciousness which would enable you to live more creatively.

— A more sensitive awareness of the risen Christ shaping your hours and days.

— A deeper sense of your own inward unity which would enable you to make a more powerful contribution towards enriching the life of the community(ies) to which you belong.

COMMUNITY DEVELOPMENT

Read Romans 12:9–21

Key verse: **Love must be completely sincere. Hate what is evil, hold on to what is good.** (9)

Just try to imagine a 'down-to-earth' community (a church?), living in the world as we know it, but which is inspired by all that these verses suggest!

☐ *Loving* (9). This is the heart of the matter. Loving which goes beyond liking. Loving which deliberately looks for that to respect in the lives of the people we know. Loving which appreciates strengths before it criticizes weaknesses.

☐ *Forgiving* (14). This really is asking a great deal. People do act negatively towards us. Some do seek to destroy our reputations and cast doubts on our sincerity. How do we react positively to such people? Think again about what you read in chapter two and relate it to community life.

☐ *Identifying* (15). In moments of acute need we know the people who really care. They hold on tightly to us. Their tears mingle with ours. They are ready to be inconvenienced and even to suffer for us. Are we that kind of people? Am I that kind of person?

☐ *Positive living* (21). There is evil about. It does affect all our lives. The greatest harm it can do to us is so to demean us that we sink to the same level as those who perpetuate it, and seek to repay in the same kind. Then evil really has done what it set out to do.

Reflect on the following 'word' from Martin Buber:
'Men do not find God if they stay in the world. They do not find him if they leave the world. He who goes out with his whole being to meet his THOU and carries to it all being that is in the world, finds him who cannot be sought.'
Try to re-phrase what Buber is saying and put it into your own words. It could be a rewarding exercise — even more so if you turn it into a prayer of commitment.

ON GUARD!

Read Ephesians 4:25–32
Key verse: **Don't give the Devil a chance.** (27)

Whether or not we think of the Devil in personal terms, we are all aware that evil forces are constantly at work trying to undermine the life of Christian communities. Sometimes the Devil gets his foot inside through the choir or perhaps the youth club — but in various ways and at various times he does wriggle his way inside. Our job is to make sure that our defences are as sound as we can make them, and then, when they are penetrated, that we have sufficient wisdom and strength to identify him and throw him out!

☐ *Words* (25 and 29). They come to our lips so easily and there is a certain enjoyment in knocking people off their pedestals. But words are potentially dangerous (read James 3:1–10). Of course the opposite possibilities must also be noted. Words can encourage, heal and bless.

☐ *Anger* (26). This is a necessary emotion. We all need to be angry from time to time for our psychological health's sake. Anger can lead to positive action when it is righteous anger. (Jesus was angry when he saw what the moneychangers were doing in the Temple.) But often we get angry for selfish reasons and such anger can easily lead to destructive actions. It is always a good idea to ask ourselves why we are angry. What is the direct reason for this deep feeling to be aroused? When we recognize this without distortion, we can deal with it adequately.

☐ *Other feelings* (31). Paul is right to want to see an end to unproductive ways of behaviour. But how do we get rid of bitterness and hatred? The previous verse gives the answer. It refers to 'the expulsive power of a new affection'. The Holy Spirit is the instrument of our deliverance.

Elizabeth O'Connor in 'Our Many Selves' (Harper and Row USA) writes:
'Perhaps the sufferings of the Church today will take her into her own desert experience, in which there will come a unifying of those four dimensions of corporate existence which have becomed severed from each other. These are the dimensions of community, self, God and the world.'

She also writes in the same book: 'We become individuals in relation to others and where there is no community the self is damaged and grows in crooked ways'.

Do these thoughts and this Bible passage have anything to say to your experience in the community, with yourself, with God, and out in the world? If so write them down and pray them in.

A PEOPLE PREPARED

Read John 17:6–19
Key verse: '... **so they may be one just as you and I are one.**' (11)

The hour of testing is soon to come. Jesus prays for his disciples. This is all that he can do for them now but he does so with confidence. He has been working on this team of men for some time now. All the while he has been thinking about the hour of parting. How would they fare when his physical presence was taken away from them? Would his reminders that he was always going to be with them and available to meet their needs, have got through?

The events that lay ahead would test them in two ways. First of all they would be tested as individuals. We know how some of them had to learn the lesson of failure before they set their feet on the way to success. But the other test was to be a test of their community life; of their fellowship; of their love for one another. The future of his mission was in God's hands but God had directed Jesus to this band of men who were to be the advance guard; the pioneers; the forerunners. How had he tried to equip them?

☐ *By experience.* He had sent them out to do their own thing. He had entrusted them with a variety of tasks. Then they had returned. On their return they talked with Jesus about what had happened. They reflected upon their experience. (See Mark 9:28–29, Luke 10:17–24.) From these 'case histories' they began to make discoveries both about themselves and about the way they functioned. This was extremely valuable. Just as medical students must spend time on the wards seeing sickness at first hand, so the Lord's disciples had to come face to face with reality. It was a hard school but it was necessary.

☐ *By prayer.* As they went out Jesus went with them. Not always through his physical presence, but by his deep concern for them which he expressed through prayer. He wanted them to be one because he knew that by their 'oneness' they would bear an effective witness.

Think over the key verse again. Would it be reasonable to suggest a revised translation: 'That they may be whole just as you and I are whole'? What might this imply?
— *Our personal 'wholeness' is affected by the quality of our relationships.*
— *Our corporate 'wholeness' is a vital factor in mission.*

·

IF GEESE CAN DO IT . . .!

Read Ephesians 1:15–23

Key verse: The church is Christ's body, the completion of him who himself completes all things everywhere. (23)

At Tubingen in 1964 the World Council of Churches convened a conference to discuss 'The Healing Church'. One of the speakers told the members that when geese make their long migration journeys they always fly in V formation. And this is for a purpose. Each bird, except for the leader, finds uplift in the vacuum created by the bird ahead. As the lead bird tires so another bird takes the leader's place. By this means they can maintain speeds of up to 100 kilometres an hour. Then if one bird becomes especially tired and has to go to ground, another bird automatically goes with it to give support and to enable them both eventually to reach their destination. He ended the illustration with this telling phrase: 'If geese can do it . . .!

It is easy to despair of the church as we know it. The organization creaks. It acts so slowly. It has become so fragmented. It often appears timid and tired. That is the negative side and it must not be forgotten.

But the positive side is here in this passage. There is surely a church within the church as we know it. A church which bears no name but that of Christ. It is comprehensive and wide in its embrace, but it is marked by certain qualities and it enjoys marvellous privileges. Paul lists here the blessings enjoyed by 'the church which is Christ's body'. It offers light to the mind and hope for the future. It is characterized by the same mighty power that raised up Jesus from the dead, and finally it offers 'completion', which is surely another word for one we have used frequently in these pages — 'wholeness'.

Now the proof of the reality of our participating in these gifts and blessings will lie in whether or not we do as the geese do — live for each other; sustain one another in crisis; lift each other when there is danger of falling, and go down into the depths with each other when we do fall. If geese can do it . . .!

T.S. Eliot wrote:
>*For us there is only the trying,*
>*the rest is not our business.*

Yes, but it is 'his' business. As we try he stands by us to make our poor efforts 'complete'. And because of this we cannot only try — we can fly!

PARTING GIFT

Read 2 Corinthians 13:11–13

Key verse: **The grace of our Lord Jesus Christ, the love of God and the fellowship of the Holy Spirit be with you all.** (13)

If we are to bring healing to divided communities we must be well equipped. This is God's promise given to us through Paul. We are the heirs and successor of the Corinthian Christians. Our faith is their faith. The promise is for us.

☐ *The grace of our Lord Jesus Christ.* Grace is God's love in action. It is God taking the initiative on our behalf. Count Zinzendorf, the Moravian leader, called for missionaries to go to the new world. There was only one snag. They could only get near to the people who needed them most if they became slaves. Tobias Leopold and Leonard Dober immediately volunteered and were sold into slavery. This was just what Jesus did for us; and it was and is — all of grace!

☐ *The love of God.* How easy to build up a wrong picture of God and see him as a kind of celestial policeman who watches over us and writes down all our grievous errors. God is not like that. His love works for our highest welfare. It is our ultimate guarantee as John Wesley realized when, on his death bed, he said, 'The best of all — God is with us'.

☐ *And the fellowship of the Holy Spirit.* This simply means that God is here and now. The life of God is in the soul of man.

> And every virtue we possess,
> And every conquest won,
> And every thought of holiness,
> Are his alone. (Harriet Auber)

God is not 'out there'; he is 'in here'. Through our relationships with others who share our faith we are being shaped and moulded. The Holy Spirit is alive through our fellowship with them.

AN ACT OF DEDICATION

Christ behind me

In the past. All that has been good is in his keeping. All that was bad, shameful and hurtful, I consign to the depths of his mercy.

Christ before me

He is the Way stretching before me from where I am now. I face the future knowing that my best way is his way.

Christ beside me

His strong shoulder is under every burden I carry. Nothing can separate me from his love.

Christ beneath me

'Underneath are the everlasting arms.' When I fall he lifts me up. His strength undergirds my weakness.

Christ above me

His love spreads over me. I claim his protection. Under the shadow of his wings I trust and at night I sleep in peace.

Christ within me

'I live, yet not I, but Christ lives in me.' By the bread which is broken and the wine which is poured out, I know that you, Lord, are within me. Therefore when I am weak, then I am strong.

HEALING AND COMMUNITY
Suggestions for group work

1. Are there any particular community factors in your area which seem to affect health standards adversely? List them and ask yourselves what is being done about them and if anything more could be done.

2. Are you familiar with the work of the local Community Health Council? Ask for a copy of its annual report in advance of the meeting. Are there ways in which you could become usefully involved?

3. A local church put a poster outside its doors which read — 'THIS CHURCH IS A HEALTH CENTRE'. In what ways and by what means does a church community promote health? Can you think of practical ways in which your church(es) could get involved? Should you be thinking of making suggestions to your Church Council, P.C.C. or Elders Meeting?

4. Now that you have come to the end of this short series, do you consider that your group has been a 'sharing and caring group'? Will you miss it now that the series is over? We should not just have meetings for meetings' sake but is there a place for 'caring and sharing' on a more regular basis? And what about prayer groups which concentrate on helping people who are ill — should there be such a representative group in your church(es)?

The Bible Reading Fellowship

● encourages regular, informed Bible-reading as a means of renewal in the churches

● issues various series of regular Bible readings with explanatory notes

● publishes introductory booklets on Bible-reading, group study guides, training aids, audio-visual material, etc.

Write or call now for full list of publications.

The Bible Reading Fellowship

St Michael's House	P.O. Box M	All Saints Parish
2 Elizabeth Street	Winter Park	P.O. Box 328
London SW1W 9RQ	Florida 32790	Dickson ACT 2602
	USA	Australia